Images of War

THE CENTRAL POWERS
ON THE RUSSIAN FRONT
1914–1918

David Bilton

Pen & Sword
MILITARY

First published in Great Britain in 2014 by
PEN & SWORD MILITARY
an imprint of
Pen & Sword Books Ltd,
47 Church Street,
Barnsley,
South Yorkshire,
S70 2AS

A CIP record for this book is available from the British Library.

ISBN 978 1 78340 053 9

Pen & Sword Books Ltd incorporates the Imprints of
Pen & Sword Aviation, Pen & Sword Maritime,
Pen & Sword Military, Wharncliffe Local History, Pen & Sword Select,
Pen & Sword Military Classics and Leo Cooper.

For a complete list of Pen & Sword titles please contact
Pen & Sword Books Limited
47 Church Street, Barnsley, South Yorkshire, S70 2AS, England

E-mail: enquiries@pen-and-sword.co.uk
Website: www.pen-and-sword.co.uk

Contents

Acknowledgements

As with previous books, a great big thank you to Anne Coulson for her help in checking the text and to The Prince Consort's Library for all their help.
Errors of omission or commission are mine alone.

Introduction

This book covers the fighting and very briefly, where relevant, the politics and economics of the war in Russia. In such a slender photographic tome it is not possible to cover every event, even in the timeline. Therefore the main focus is on the Habsburg and Hohenzollern Empires' troops in Russia. The photographs used in this book come from a private collection and texts published at the time.

The size, complexity, contradictions of success and the sheer confusion of the fighting on the Russian Front are clearly shown by the following extracts, all from one month in 1915: 'Varying fortunes on rest of front. Fall of Grodno. Russians re-enter Grodno. Russians retreat towards Minsk. Germans retire in Rovno region. German advance comes to a standstill nearly all along line, though Russians still retiring slowly. Scattered fighting along most of the line, except Dvinsk.' And with losses running into the tens of thousands who could tell if they were really winning at any given moment?

Pre-war plans had been formulated round the offensive, so the fighting of August was based on great offensives: pre-war illusions in which the defensive was ignored. It was a war of movement that would be over by Christmas. The German plan was based upon a slow Russian mobilisation which gave them a window of opportunity to beat the French before turning on the Russians.

The fighting soon turned into siege warfare on the Western Front, with offensive manoeuvre only returning in 1918. In the East the situation remained more fluid. Fighting a war of movement, often over long distances, there was little time for the development of a trench system as complex as those on the Western Front. Many positions were therefore temporary, as the fighting usually centred around 'communications hubs like highway crossings, forts and railway stations'. In fact, some areas did have intricate trench systems like those on the Western Front, but in the majority of sectors they were temporary. 'But the essential reasons for the eastern front's remaining for so long a place of manoeuvre, not of Stellungskrieg, were the lower defensive fire-power and the lesser mobility of reserves than in the west.'

An Englishman, John Morse, serving with the Russian Army in 1914 commented on the difference between the eastern and western trenches. 'The Allies' and the German trenches are said to often be within a few yards of each other, this was seldom the case in the East. There was generally a considerable space between the two lines: here near Skyermevice it amounted to 3,000 yards.' One reason he believed to be a cause of this difference 'was the extreme hardness of the earth, which made it impossible to dig fresh trenches during the winter-time'. There were similarities between the west and east. One was the German fear of franc-tireurs, and the punishment they received, as at Louvain (Leuven) in Belgium, which was sacked and burned because of supposed franc-tireur activity. Harsh reprisals also happened in Poland. Kalisch on the Silesian border was shelled into oblivion on 14 August after snipers had supposedly fired on German troops. The population were also fined 27,000 roubles for the offence. 'The Russians began a policy of forcible "russification" as they advanced into Galicia, driving Jews from their homes and forcibly converting churches to Orthodoxy.'

A further similarity was the refugee, although in greater numbers in the east. It is estimated that there were 3.5 million refugees moving into central Russia by 1915, as many as 7.4 million by July 1917. Many moved as a result of Austro-German offensives, but others were forcibly deported by the Russians, particularly ethnic Germans and Jews.

Unlike in the west, cavalry had a role to play and was regularly used to exploit situations and attack on its own. Cossacks and German cavalry alike behaved both bravely and badly, with both sides burning villages and slaying villagers in a tit-for-tat way.

Another difference with the west was in communications. In the east the side that moved the fastest usually had the advantage and generally that advantage was won by the efficient and effective German staff system.

Although small in number, a very important difference between Russia and all other fighting powers was the Russian use of women in war. 'Between 5,000 and 6,000 women had been enlisted for combat by November 1917. The best known unit was the so-called Battalion of Death (Zenski batal 'Smerti) raised by the Provisional Government and led by Maria Botchkareva, known as 'Yashka', a butcher's daughter whose husband had been killed at the front.'

As well as enormously long distances, so also were the numbers involved huge. Calling-up the 1914 class would provide a Russian army of over seven million, with a general staff, alone among all the major combatants in having had experience of fighting a modern war – the Russo-Japanese war, though one which it had lost. Although rich in men, it was lacking in equipment and incapable of maintaining even a fraction of its potential strength as a fully functioning force under the conditions of modern warfare.

The situation was similar in the Austro-Hungarian Army. It was under-equipped and lacking in guns at all levels. As in the Russian Army, there were not even enough rifles. They 'could not produce rifles fast enough to equip the empire's rapidly expanding armed forces' and handle its battlefield attrition. This resulted in the use of obsolete types, captured equipment and cancelled foreign gun orders: a quartermaster's nightmare for parts and ammunition types.

Another combatant in poor shape for a war was the Ottoman Empire which 'was unwilling to enter the war until November … its army was incapable of combat operations until December 1914'. Unlike the German Schlieffen Plan, the French Plan Seventeen and the Russian double Plan A and G, it 'had no clearly defined war aims, nor did peacetime Turkish war plans in 1914 call for any offensive operations against neighbouring countries'. While the other combatants had cheered the decision for war, there was no enthusiasm in Turkey. 'For the Turks, 1914 was not a year of cheering crowds sending off troop trains of patriotic soldiers to the front. Instead, 1914 was a year of respite and recovery from the disastrous Balkan Wars of 1912 and 1913.'

'For the Turkish General Staff and for the Turkish Army, 1914 was supposed to be a year devoted to the rebuilding of an army shattered by war'. As in the Russian Army, there was a shortage of every type of equipment, but unlike that army which it was to fight, there was also a manpower shortage. The estimated mobilisation potential of 2,000,000 was never realised. However, this shortage of men did not stop the Turkish Army sending troops to assist its Central Powers partners when asked. In 1916 it sent two divisions to Galicia, three to Romania and two to Macedonia.

The only army that was fully equipped was the dominant partner of the Central Powers: Germany. Its divisions were well-trained and at full war establishment with suitable reserves. It had sufficient industrial capacity to replenish stocks and it was incontestably superior in high-trajectory artillery. Manpower was its problem a problem, exacerbated by a war on two fronts. Its priority initially was the Western Front so resources were concentrated there, leaving a minimal presence in the east which the Russians were able to exploit.

In August 1914 things went much as had been expected. 'There were great offensives: the Schlieffen Plan set the bulk of Moltke's army marching through Belgium into the French Flank; Plan XVII set most of Joffre's army attacking German positions in Alsace and Lorraine; Plan No. 19 set two Russian armies against East Prussia, and four others against Austrian Galicia; the Austro-Hungarian army also attacked both Serbia and Russia.'

On all the fronts, there were massive strategic manoeuvres, bringing the Germans far into France, the Russians far into Austria; in East Prussia, there was a great encounter between the German VIII Army and the two Russian armies, in which troops marched and counter-marched…until one of the Russian armies was resoundingly defeated in the battle of Tannenberg (25th-30th August), and the other expelled from East Prussia in the Battle of the Masurian Lakes (7th-14th September).

In terms of numbers, by mid-1917, 1,528 German battalions faced 2,403 Russo-Romanian battalions. In distance terms it 'was calculated that one and a half German divisions occupied in the east space that would have absorbed five divisions in the west; the Austrians similarly calculated that they had one rifle for two metres of front in the east, whereas they had three rifles for every metre on their Italian Front'. Each side had around 8,000 guns in the east but in the west the Entente had 18,000 to 11,000 German guns. This lack of men left large gaps in the line that could be exploited when troops became available.

Along with the huge numbers of combatants were huge numbers of prisoners, casualties and deaths, around 2,000,000 dead and missing German and Austro-Hungarians against 2,200,000 dead, missing and deserting Russians. The numbers of wounded and prisoners were even bigger – whole divisions surrendered at a time: 'I arrived in captivity with my whole division' wrote one Hungarian officer, 'with its soldiers, with its officers, with its commanders and even its heavy artillery.' An estimated 2.7 million Austro-Hungarian soldiers, one third of the number mobilised, were captured, of whom about 2,000,000 fell into Russian hands, mostly between 1914 to 1916. This is very much higher than for the German Army which recorded only 167,000 men as Russian POWs.

'Open combat was usually far more bloodier than static fighting' so casualty rates were higher on the Eastern Front. In the west, the German Army 'sustained its heaviest battle casualties during the three-month war of movement in 1914 and suffered grievously again during the mobile fighting in March 1918. In the east during the early stages of the conflict, battle losses far exceeded those in the west. The highest casualty rate experienced by the German army during the First World War on any front was that of the 1914-15 campaign in East Prussia and Poland, where losses amounted to 476 wounded per 1,000 men. Against this figure, the casualties from the more famous western trench warfare and attritional battles of 1916 and 1917, at 182-3 wounded per 1,000 men, appear positively modest.' But due to the smaller number of artillery guns in the east and therefore less shelling, the mobile nature of the war meant that troops in the east had fewer psychological problems than those in the west.

It was war on a vast scale and sometimes at temperatures where men froze to death. It was a very different war from that experienced by combatants in the west.

As this book is about the Central Powers in Russia, the Russian Civil War is outside its remit. However, this did affect the Germans and Austrians, who supplied the White forces with arms and at times fought the Reds, especially in Finland and the Ukraine.

This book deals with the conflict between the main protagonists on the main front: Finland down to Romania. The other fronts will be dealt with in another book. Throughout the book Central Powers' units are identified by italics and Russian troops by standard lettering.

A Russian farmer's family in their house. A deeply religious people, even in the squalor they have an icon on the wall.

During the breakthrough in East Galicia, the Kaiser pays one of his many visits to the front. This time along the River Strypa, well ahead of his retinue.

The centre of Milau in Kurland during the war. Life continues even though there is a war on. On the left of the market place is the Kurland Hotel and on the right is the Stadtsparkasse (City Savings Bank).

Erbeutetes russisches Flugboot. (Gnome Motor 150 PS.)

A trophy of war on display: a Russian flying boat powered by a French Gnome motor. The aircraft is named Nikolajitsch. On the right is another captured plane.

Nr. 33. Geflüchtete Polen.

As is often the case, civilians get caught up in the battles and are forced to flee. These are Polish refugees.

Life was harsh for the average Russian: wrapped in rags to keep warm.

Chapter 1
1914
The opening moves

'On Monday 20 July 1914, with the guns of St Petersburg reverberating in salute, the French president, Raymond Poincaré, arrived in the Gulf of Finland aboard the Battleship *France* for a three-day visit to Russia.' Both countries were tied by a treaty of commerce and a convention whereby they would assist each other militarily in the event of a German attack. In 1905 France had entered into the Entente Cordiale with Britain. Two years later this became a triple alliance when Russia joined the Entente. The other power bloc in Europe consisted of Austria-Hungary and Germany, later joined by Italy to form the Triple Alliance.

By the summer a rough and ready balance of power appeared to have been achieved, and even signs of goodwill were displayed. Although France saw Germany as antagonistic and worked assiduously to perfect the defensive arrangements with her associates, the battleship *France* had participated in the international celebrations marking the widening of the Kiel Canal. A few days later the Archduke Franz Ferdinand and his wife the Duchess of Hohenberg were assassinated at Sarajevo. Neither Poincaré or Tsar Alexander saw this as a reason to 'imperil the new climate of confidence. Germany, they considered, could only be bluffing in supporting the Austrian demarche against Serbia'.

On 1 August, at 1700 hours, the Kaiser signed the formal order to mobilise. *16 Infantry Division* was ordered to cross into Luxembourg and the event was toasted with champagne. That evening, the German Ambassador in St Petersburg drove to the office of the Russian Foreign Minister, Sergei Sazonov, to deliver the declaration of war.

In the streets, where for days there had been barricades and demonstrations and strikes, the mood changed. Down came the barricades and the demonstrators joined the cheering crowds outside the French, Belgian and Serbian embassies. Waving flags and singing they marched to the Winter Palace. When the Tsar and Tsarina appeared on the balcony, the crowds fell on their knees and broke into the national anthem.

Throughout the night of 31 July and the next day, Berliners had waited for the general mobilisation order. The appearance of the Chancellor, heading to the Royal Palace holding a document, indicated to the crowd that mobilisation was about to be declared. With the nearby cathedral bells tolling for a war service, the crowds flocked to the Palace gates where a policeman announced mobilisation.

'The massed assembly thereupon broke into the hymn "Now thank we all our God".' 'The tension of recent days was relaxed…and Berlin's cafés, dance halls and theatres, almost empty for a week, were as full as at the season's height.' It was the same in Vienna. Flags waved, music boomed and processions formed in the street. As in Germany, many rushed to the colours as volunteers just to be part of it.'

It was more than war: 'it was a duel to the death between Slavism and Germanism' with the Tsar swearing before the miracle-working icon in the cathedral of Our Lady of Kazan that he would not 'make peace so long as there is a single enemy on Russia's soil'. The German embassy was ransacked and official German language court titles were replaced by Russian equivalents. St Petersburg was no longer a suitable name: it was replaced by Petrograd.

Following its mobilisation plans the Russian Army went to war. 'White-uniformed bands were followed by great columns of infantry; artillery and limbers rattled over the cobbles, succeeded by ambulances, transport wagons and the endless tinkle and clatter of cavalry.' The troops sped on their way by citizens who poured from the shops to watch and cheer, office workers who called and waved from windows, and families who handed them gifts as they passed. Thousands rushed to volunteer for service: men in the army and women in the hospitals.

In a war of attack and counter-attack over distances so immense, both sides were confident of victory. Russia had gone to war to stop the Austrians, the Austrians to stop the Serbians, and the Germans to aid their ally. The Triple Entente would then be drawn into the conflict. It would first be a major European war but the colonial dimensions of the protagonists would turn it into a de facto world war.

On 3 August Germany declared war on France. Germany would fight a war on two fronts, concentrating on the Western one first. On the western frontier were seven armies which by 17 August were ready to move. Although working in co-operation with the Austrians, the number of troops guarding the eastern frontier was much smaller. *IX. Reserve Korps* was only there until 23 August when the total number of available troops would be 250,000: 'three active corps and three reserve divisions, assisted by a cavalry division, one Ersatz division and Landwehr formations'.

When, on 4 August, Britain received no reply to its ultimatum demanding that Germany withdraw from Belgium, the third party of the Triple Entente entered the war. Italy would not fulfil its obligations because it was an offensive war, leaving Austria-Hungary and Germany to fight against the French, Belgians, British, Serbians and Russians. In numbers alone, the Allied nations were well ahead. By itself the Russian Army could field more men than its two opponents together.

But numbers, while impressive to the other nations, were only part of the story. Russian railways in the west used the same gauge as the Austro-Germans giving their enemy a transportation advantage. Russian trains coming from the east used a different gauge so everything had to be transferred, increasing the time taken to move men and materiel. The Russians had fewer rail lines and insufficient stock to move their armies about. They could not rely on motorised transport because the army possessed fewer than 700 vehicles with a civilian reserve of under 500. The number of field guns was half the proportion found in the German Army: with heavy guns it ran to 1/6th. Shell allocation was under half the target and cartridge production was half the known requirement. The infantry had one rifle for two men; there were fewer than 300 aircraft, a few dirigibles and only one anti-aircraft battery, which spent its time at the Tsar's safe quarters fifteen miles south of Petrograd.

Serious issues arose concerning poor training, illiteracy and personal initiative. A shortage of NCOs in the peacetime army was compounded by active service losses, leading to regimental training schools behind the line. 'There was an average of two NCOs per company in the Russian Army compared with…twelve in the German Army'. Infantry and artillery units suffered a similar shortage of officers. Many officers cared little for the well-being of their men or for their own safety: they were killed in droves in the initial months of the war. At a higher level, the generals were often old and unimaginative, hidebound by bureaucracy. And then there was endemic corruption at all levels.

Little wonder that the German plans concentrated on beating the French first and the Russians second. It presumed that the Russians would take at least six weeks to mobilise their forces and begin to move west. Virtually no German leader 'could imagine a scenario whereby the Russians could mobilise, deploy and fight well enough in the war's opening weeks and months to influence German strategy and operations in Western Europe. If the Schlieffen Plan did not work the eastern part of Germany would be exposed to a Russian advance'.

When war broke out, seven of Germany's eight field armies headed west. Only *Eighth Army* in East Prussia faced the Russians. Below them was the Polish Salient, Russian territory and further south were four Austrian armies. Like the Germans they relied on a slow Russian mobilisation so that they could eliminate Serbia first, then Russia.

Although Russian mobilisation had gone well and the population understood the need for the war and were generally behind the decision, it was a staged process: units would deploy into the field as soon as they were ready to do so. This provided a constant stream of men but there were no guarantees as to when they would be available. A simultaneous attack from the north and south across the Polish Salient would probably have removed the Salient and the Russian presence in Poland.

By 1 September, Russia had ninety divisions available in Europe and twenty more in the Caucasus theatre. The Russian high command decided to launch an attack on East Prussia and bring forward operations against the Carpathian fortifications that protected the agricultural heartland of the Austro-Hungarian empire. This was at a time when the Germans and Austro-Hungarians were facing west and south respectively.

Poor Russian communication meant that, once an attack was launched, there was little the commander could do to influence events. Orders from the general staff, in outdated code, went from Moscow to Warsaw, then to the front commander by courier and then to the army commander. In a war of movement headquarters moved, making delivery even more difficult. Acknowledgement followed the same path in reverse. Success would be determined by the quality of the commanders and co-ordination between them.

Geography conspired to help the defending German Army. The Augustovo Forest and the Masurian Lakes acted as northern and southern barriers, splitting the Russian First and Second Armies and stopping any mutual support until they had advanced 240Km to the west. Personality would also play its part. The two army commanders disliked each other and were not on speaking terms; neither liked the front commander. Local knowledge was another factor in the favour of the defenders, who had been in the area for years. Neither Generals Rennenkampf nor Samsonov knew that they were being drawn into a trap.

General von Prittwitz ordered his troops to withdraw so the Russians encountered little resistance until a message, broadcast without codes, indicated that the Russians were to rest. As a result *1.Korps* attacked what was assumed to be the main Russian force at Gumbinnen and two further corps followed. However, these were merely the advance guard and, when the Germans moved east, they found themselves outnumbered and outgunned. The three corps withdrew, leaving more than 6,000 men in Russian hands. Prittwitz's decision was a further withdrawal behind the River Vistula. On informing the Commander-in-Chief, he was ordered to stop the withdrawal. Prittwitz and his staff were replaced by Hindenburg and Ludendorff.

Plans were immediately drawn up to counter the Russian threat. Another un-coded message was intercepted and made it clear that neither Russian army could help the other. When Russian intelligence suggested that they would meet little resistance, the scene was set for another German victory.

Ludendorff urged action. Leaving a cavalry division to hold back the reticent Russian First Army, the remainder of *Eighth Army* encircled the Russian Second Army. When a Russian corps, advancing without support, was smashed by a German corps lying in wait, the army commander ordered a general withdrawal. This was not possible, being, as they were, completely cut off. There was no alternative but surrender. Second Army virtually ceased to exist: 30,000 were dead and around 100,000 were made prisoner. German casualties were less than 20,000. This was the Battle of Tannenberg.

German confidence was high. *Eighth Army* was reinforced and headed north, while the Russians expected them to head south to Warsaw. The Russian commander, realising the position his troops were in, ordered a retreat into Russia, evacuating East Prussia. With Russian losses at around 150,000, this was another German victory – The Battle of the Masurian Lakes.

Set against the setbacks in the west, the eastern victories were welcome news for the home front and to many officers, suggesting that defence in the west and attacks in the east to remove the Russian threat was the way forward. Once Russia was beaten, there would be enough troops to break the deadlock in the west. But, back in their homeland, the Russians reorganised and replaced their losses.

In the south, faced by cautious Russian commanders and a more slowly mobilising army, the Austro-Hungarians decided the best defence would be an offensive to clear Galicia and secure the mountain pass approaches. With a new German army being formed in the Cracow area, three Austrian armies moved east. This was initially a success, but when the armies started to diverge, a gap was created between them. When the Austro-Hungarian *Third Army* ran into a trap, *Fourth Army* was ordered to change its route. This created a gap between it and *First Army* which the Russians were quick to exploit. A retreat was ordered, a retreat that surrendered all their gains and more; a retreat that put them up against the Carpathian Mountains. 'The Russians could now advance unhindered towards the fortresses of Lemberg and Przemysl...the gateways to the Carpathian Mountain passes and the keys to the unfettered use of the railways of Galicia'.

Before the Russians attacked, many thousands, mostly Slavs, deserted. When the Russians did attack, many willingly surrendered. As the army pulled westwards, Lemberg was left on its own with little chance of help. There was ample food and ammunition for a reasonable defence of the city but the arrival of many thousands of dispirited troops 'sent the city into a paroxysm of fear'. Some units had offered resistance but the remnants of five corps converged on the city.

After an artillery bombardment, Russian troops moved into the city's suburbs. Many of the troops available for the defence were Slavs who threw down their guns and walked to the Russian lines; the non-Slavs retreated west. Lemberg fell on 3 September without a shot being fired. An estimated 130,000 men were taken prisoner. Like the German success in East Prussia, the capture of so many came with their equipment: 700 artillery pieces, 2,000 machine guns, 500,000 rifles, tons of food and mountains of ammunition. The non-military prizes were probably more important; they gave the Russians control of the region's most important railway hub, rolling stock and the most important locomotive factory in Galicia.

The Austro-Hungarians, with fresh troops, set up a new defensive line near Grodek anchored on the River San. However, when the Russians moved against Jaroslav on the San they voluntarily withdrew, surrendering the entire river and the railroad from Cracow to Przemysl, a fortress complex. This gave the Russians command of the northern approaches to the fortress and when Brusilov's men took Grodek the Russians were in a very favourable position to take Przemysl. The capture of the fortress would allow them to approach the Carpathian Mountain passes into Hungary and also German Silesia.

Przemysl was in a stronger position than Lemberg. With more modern guns, a high-grade garrison, sufficient food and ammunition for months, it was expected to withstand a siege for at least eight months. Lacking sufficiently heavy artillery to damage the fort, and finding considerable resistance to their attacks, the Russians decided to put defences on the approaches to Przemysl to stop any relief. They then moved in the direction of Cracow in attempt to get there before the Germans could set up their defences.

By mid-September there were sufficient reinforcements in Poland to form the *Ninth Army*. The plan was to push through the centre of the Polish Salient and take Warsaw before winter. One German army faced three Russian armies, who, unable to form a solid defensive line, chose to defend the major river crossings. The tactic was effective: German attempts to cross the Vistula near Novogeorgievsk and near Ivangorod were turned back by Russian heavy artillery. Following this, a Russian attack pushed the Germans back from the Vistula and inflicted huge casualties at Kozienice.

In response, Zeppelins were sent to bomb Warsaw. Finding that it did not have the desired effect on the population and after the loss of one to Russian guns, their use was discontinued.

As in the west, the machine gun was king of the eastern battlefield. Using conventional tactics to get close, never mind into the opposing trenches, was difficult and costly. This was particularly so for the Russians who mounted their attacks in overwhelming numbers in the old style of frontal attack - wave after wave.

Karl von Wiegand, a reporter for United Press, witnessed the Russian attack at the battle of Wirballen in Russian Poland. 'On came the Slav swarm – into the range of the German trenches, with wild yells and never a waver. Russian battle flags…appeared in the front of the charging ranks. The advance line thinned and the second line moved up. Nearer and nearer they swept towards the German positions.' Then the machine guns opened fire. 'I saw a sudden, almost grotesque, melting of the advancing lines. It was different to anything that had taken place before. The men literally went down like dominoes in a row. Those who kept their feet were hurled back as though by a terrible gust of wind.' Then the men following faltered. 'Mounted officers dashed along the line urging the men forward. Horses fell with the men. In the face of such a volume of fire the line broke. Panic ensued. It was every man for himself. The entire Russian charge turned and went tearing back to cover and the shelter of the Russian trenches.'

The machine gun had triumphed and in less than a couple of minutes there were only two types of Russians still on the battlefield. 'The dead were everywhere. They were not piled up, but were strewn over acres. More horrible than the sight of the dead…squirming, tossing, writhing figures everywhere! The wounded.'

Initially successful in their renewed attack on Warsaw, the German attackers were eventually stopped by the strength of the Russian artillery and the sheer number of their troops. The arrival of Siberian reinforcements, followed by ample stocks of ammunition and food, resulted in a German retreat.

Hindenburg's response was to subsume Austro-Hungarian divisions into the German *Ninth Army* ready for another attack on Warsaw. The Russians believed the Central Powers were in full retreat so they attacked at the junction of the German and Austro-Hungarian armies near Kielce, successfully pushing the Austro-Hungarians back. By 10 November they had almost cleared the salient of the Central Powers.

The Russians were ready to deliver their next attack. Berlin was only 200 miles away. However, their advance had created gaps between units and the supply train could not keep up. On 11 November Mackensen launched a flank attack on Rennenkampf's First Army taking thousands of prisoners. Second Army was ordered to Lodz along with thousands of reinforcements to prevent the Germans trapping Second Army. Marching through a snowstorm, Fifth Army was at Lodz in just two days: a distance of seventy miles. There were now seven corps in and around the city.

The Russians now attempted to encircle the Germans but, when one German corps broke through and attacked from the rear, the Russians retreated. Leaving Lodz to the Germans, they retreated to Warsaw. With winter approaching and insufficient troops, Hindenburg was unable to follow the Russians.

The fighting, sniping and skirmishing continued throughout the winter. Even deep snow did not stop hostile activities. The German Army adopted white suits to allow movement in no-man's-land; this the Russians copied.

White suits allowed German troops to get close to the Russian wire unseen unless the sentries were especially vigilant. John Morse saw a white shape come to their wire and work out where the exit points were. Joined by others, they inspected the wire and searched the dead. They withdrew as soon as the Russians opened fire.

John Morse also experienced the use of subterfuge to try to enter the Russian trenches. He had read about Germans posing as Englishmen on the Western Front. One night he heard a lot of noise coming towards his section. The order was to stay quiet until the last minute. As the Germans approached the Russian wire they shouted out: 'We are a reinforcement of Russians; do not fire on your comrades!' Rapid fire, followed by a bayonet charge, removed the threat.

The year for both sides was easy to sum up. Two large Russian armies, poorly equipped, gallantly but ineptly led, had immediately attacked East Prussia. 'Although ultimately disastrous, their misguided onslaught did serve to force the Germans to withdraw forces from the West at a critical time. Hindenburg crushed the Russians at Tannenberg.' However, the Russian invasion of Galicia had proved less easy to contain but was eventually blocked a few miles east of Cracow.

'The campaigns of 1914 exhausted nearly all the available German stocks of war material. It was little comfort that Germany's antagonists had endured still higher coasts and losses, for these countries commanded resources that were vastly superior.' Germany now faced a long war that it had tried hard to avoid.

Captured Uhlans being escorted to the rear during the early days of the war.

Few units took their regimental standards to war as they had done in previous times. Their loss was bad for morale and good propaganda for the enemy. Here Russian soldiers show off a captured Austrian standard.

Above: **The speed of the Austrian retreat meant that there was no time to take heavy equipment with them. Here four Austrian field guns have been captured and if their breechblock has been left behind they will be turned on their former owners.**

Left: **As well as leaving their artillery behind it was necessary for the Austrians to blow up bridges to slow down the Russian advance. This is the bridge over the Dniester.**

Left: **Tens of thousands of Austrians were taken prisoner. Here, a solitary Russian guards two of them. Neither looks concerned about the future.**

Below: **German troops during the advance on Warsaw. The roads are un-surfaced and are already starting to turn to mud.**

The un-surfaced roads quickly turned to mud when wet and became quagmires in the winter when not frozen or covered in snow.

Expecting the Russian mobilisation to be slow, most of the German Army had moved west. When the Russians attacked, much sooner than anticipated, troops had to be transferred quickly to the east. These soldiers have just arrived in East Prussia direct from the Western Front.

The retreating Russian Army lost much of its equipment. This was carefully gathered up for show as war trophies and for issuing to second line troops. Much went to the Austrian Army that had a continual shortage of guns. This war salvage is on show in the East Prussian town of Plotzen.

Captured Russian soldiers on their arrival at Neu-Ulm in Germany on 25 November 1914.

German officer with binoculars, sword and Iron Cross Second Class, posing in his private purchase winter coat. The card is dated 26 December 1914 and was sent to his family.

Captured Russian field gun displayed as a trophy in front of the Emperor's castle in Berlin. A member of *3 Foot Guard Regiment* posted this card on 20 October 1914 from Berlin.

Aufstellung einer eroberten russischen Kanone vor dem Königl. Schloß in Berlin.

A German captive somewhere in Siberia. He has already acquired some of the extra clothing he will need to survive in the bitter cold of Siberia.

Die Russen ergeben sich

'The Russians arise' is the caption for this photograph of Russian troops surrendering.

Newly captured Russian officers, one of whom appears to be wearing a German cavalry helmet.

Gruppe russischer Offiziere, welche sich zum Spaß mit deutschen Uniformen bekleiden, die sie den Gefangenen abgenommen haben

The lonely grave of a soldier from *Landwehr Infantry Regiment 46* who died on 10 October 1914. This regiment was part of *3 Landwehr Division* and was primarily raised in the Prussian provinces of Posen, Lower Silesia and West Prussia. It spent the war on the Eastern Front until September 1918 when it was transferred to the west.

Stefan Rettenbacher, a twenty-nine-year-old reservist in a national protection regiment, was killed in action on 29 November 1914.

Josef Hummel, serving in *1 Company* of *5 Infantry Regiment* was born in Naisa in Bavaria on 8 December 1886. He was killed in action on 29 October 1914, during the advance on **Warsaw** while serving in *36 Infantry Division*.

Members of *4.Kompagnie, Landsturm Ersatz Bataillon No.7* relaxing somewhere in East Prussia during November 1914. The belt size of most of the men indicates why they are garrison troops.

A well-earned rest while marching through East Prussia in the first weeks of the war. The card was posted at Tapiau in the northern part of East Prussia.

Captured Russian artillery position. The man on the left is carrying a side-arm and wearing a military cap but no uniform.

Farewell. An Austrian card showing the mobilisation at the start of the war. It was posted by Josef Hüber serving in *15 Bavarian Landwehr Infantry* regiment entrenched in Lorraine.

A mixed group of Private First class and NCOs in a railway unit standing beside a newly laid track. A soldier serving with *POW railway work detachment 51* sent the card.

Honvédség (Hungarian) cavalry in late autumn in the Carpathians. In the centre, a sergeant is holding a map, flanked on either side by corporals. The weather has not broken as they are only wearing their standard uniform. They are equipped with sword and a side arm.

Tapiau in East Prussia after the Russians had left. On the left are captured Russian field cookers. Posted by a member of the *Landsturm Bataillon Muskau*, a garrison unit from Saxony.

Officers of the *Polish Legion* that was created in Galicia on 27 August and fought for the Habsburgs. Initially the Polish Legion was composed of two legions: the Eastern and the Western. After a Russian victory in the Battle of Galicia, the Eastern Polish legion refused to fight against Russia and was disbanded on 21 September. On 19 December, the Western legion was transformed into three brigades. After the creation of the puppet Kingdom of Poland, the *Polish Legion* was transferred to German command. Most refused to swear allegiance to the emperor and were interned. Approximately 3,000 of them were drafted into the Habsburg army or the German *Polnische Wehrmacht* and sent to the Italian Front, while approximately 7,500 stayed in the Austrian *Polish Auxiliary Corps*.

49 Reserve Division memorial to the men who died during the withdrawal from Lodz. 'To honour the memory of the fallen comrades in the fight between 17 and 24 November 1914'.

Artillery position in Poland. Note the lack of a spike on the top.

Constructing trenches near Warsaw.

Waving the regimental flag. Austro-Hungarian troops on the way to the front in Galicia.

Austro-Hungarian troops on the way home after fighting in Galicia.

Chapter 2
1915
The ever-changing front

'By January 1915, for the start of the Central Powers' offensive, there were seventy-nine Austro-German infantry divisions, and fifteen and a half cavalry ones, to eighty-three Russian infantry and twenty-five cavalry divisions.' By May the balance favoured the Central Powers: 109½ against just over 100 with 22½ in the Caucasus fighting against the Turks.

As well as manpower shortages in the Austro-Hungarian Army and the political fighting between the two Central Powers, another serious challenge to the Habsburg Supreme Command surfaced during the Carpathian battles. 'Growing numbers of politically unreliable Czechoslovakian, Ruthenian, and Romanian replacement troops were deployed on the Eastern Front. Their arrival coincided with an increase in antimilitary, antidynastic propaganda. Troops deserted in increasing numbers, a problem that continued throughout the Carpathian winter offensives. Among the most notorious defections was that of Czech *Infantry Regiment 28*. The regiment, recruited from industrialized Prague, reputedly crossed over to the enemy en masse "without a single shot being fired from a Russian battalion'. At no other time during the war, with the possible exception of the summer 1916 Brusilov offensive and the late October 1918 final battles of the war, had Slavic soldiers so brazenly shirked their duty as in the Carpathian Winter War.'

On 23 January, the Austro-Hungarian offensive opened with forty-one divisions to thirty-one Russian infantry and eleven cavalry. In the north an Austro-Hungarian army would seize the passes of the western Carpathians, the German *Südarmee* would capture the central passes and in the east another Austro-Hungarian army would seize the Russian flank. These operations were described by the Austrian official historians as 'a cruel folly': scaling mountains in mid-winter. 'Supply-lines were either an ice-rink or a marsh, depending on freeze or thaw; clouds hung low, and obscured the visibility of artillery-targets; shells either bounced off ice or were smothered in mud; whole bivouacs would be found frozen to death in the morning. Rifles had to be held over a fire before they could be used.' Although there was plenty of wood in the forests, there were no means to transport it.

In these situations the Russians were slightly better off than the Austro-German forces. When neither horse or motorised transport could get through, the Bactrian camel often succeeded. Used in large numbers to transport materiel, they were able to survive in temperatures as low as -40°C and could keep their footing on the most slippery ground and travel over deep snow without sinking. According to John Morse, serving with the Russians, they 'proved to be very useful throughout the winter, until the thaw came'.

On the first day of the offensive, *Third Army* took the Uzsok pass; after nearly a week of fighting *Südarmee* reached a point it had expected to be at on the first day, where their advance was stopped by fresh Russian troops. In the Bukovina, progress was better and the River Dniester was reached by mid-February.

Part of *Südarmee's* problem were the German troops. Put there to stiffen the Austro-Hungarians, they were unfamiliar with mountain conditions. They lacked the most basic winter attire and equipment, hundreds suffered frostbite every day, and many succumbed to the White Death.

Colonel Veith described his regiment's experience during battle. 'On 23 January we rushed forward into the icy hell of the Carpathian battlefield. We stormed the Uzsok, Verecke and Wyszkov Passes, but on the northern slope of the mountains, the troops encountered a blizzard. The reports from these days are shocking. Every day hundreds froze to death. The wounded that were unable to drag themselves forward were left behind to die. Entire ranks were reduced to tears in the face of the terrible agony.'

It continued like this for the whole offensive. 'Each night, the *21. Infantry Regiment* dug in until the last man was found frozen to death at daybreak. Pack animals could not advance through the deep snow. The men had to carry their own supplies on foot. The soldiers went without food for days. At -25°C, food rations froze solid. For seven days straight, the *43. Infantry Division* battled overpowering Russian troops with no warm food to sustain them. For a full thirty days, not one single man had any shelter. Hardly a battalion on the Habsburg front consisted of 200 men as lines grew thinner and thinner. Battle-weary front line troops were continuously being wrenched from one position to another to plug a newly-formed gap. Medics and those not seriously ill or injured were called into service. A constant state of mass confusion reigned; a tremendous detriment to any military command. Apathy and indifference were gaining a foothold and could not be contained.'

By this time the Austrians were exhausted and unable to hold the Russian offensive against their western side. They retreated, losing most of their gains. Colonel Veith described why this had happened. 'At the end of January, a sudden thaw and rain set in. Everyone was drenched to the bone, with no chance to dry off. Adding to this the men's clothing froze to their bodies overnight like an icy suit of armour. Those that didn't have nerves of steel broke down. Then, the Russian counter-attack struck. The soldiers, already half mad before the ordeal, retreated in apathetic resignation to their original positions. By now, even the enemy had enough of the fighting. On their side too, entire units surrendered. Finally, the killing subsided. There we were, where we had begun in mid-January; but in the time that had passed, yet another army had perished.'

Losses had been heavy, especially in professional officers and NCOs. Corps were holding the usual frontage with numbers equal only to a division. The records of two regiments stand as representative of the level of loss during the Carpathian Mountains campaign: *42 Honvéd Infantry Division's Landwehr Infantry Regiment 28* lost twenty-six officers and 1,800 enlisted men within two days (many of whom froze to death); '*Schützen* (Defence) *Regiment 20* sank from 60 officers and 34,000 men to 9 officers and 250 men after many froze to death.'

The German campaign of 1915 was to be opened with a further attempt in the central plains of the Vistula. 'At the end of January *Ninth Army* attacked, near Bolimów, using gas: its first appearance in the war. The attack went wrong – gas blew back on the Germans, and cold weather ensured that it would be…ineffective.' The Germans broke off their attack but the Russians counter-attacked with eleven divisions. With no coherent plan and little training, this attempt failed with the loss of 40,000 men in just three days.

New Austro-Hungarian divisions, many only paper formations, were sent for another offensive, an offensive prompted by the threat of a Russian invasion of Hungary, the need to liberate Przemysl and the mounting political pressure to keep Italy and Romania out of the war.

Before the Austro-Hungarians could start their offensive, intercepted Russian communications caused the Germans to advance their timetable for a second battle in the Masurian Lakes. On 7 February, in the middle of a snowstorm, Below's *Eighth Army* launched a surprise attack against General Sievers' Tenth Army 'and advanced 70 miles within the week, inflicting severe casualties on the Russians. The Russian withdrawal was disorderly and many of them were taken prisoner. The greatest loss came when the Russian 20th Army Corps, under General Bulgakov, had become surrounded by the German Tenth Army in the Augustow Forest; on February 21 the entire corps surrendered.' This allowed the rest of Tenth Army to form a new defensive position.

'The next day, Plehve's…Twelfth Army counter-attacked and checked the German advance. The counter-attack ended any further German advances and brought the battle to an end.' However, it had 'attained its primary objective of purging East Prussia of enemy presence. Another Russian army had been destroyed and significant troop numbers taken prisoner. The military success, though a tactical one, did not produce the required strategic victory and depleted the German reserve.' Exhaustion set in, 'the troops had reached the end of human endurance'.

The same was reported in the Austro-Hungarian forces: they had 'reached the extreme parameters of their physical capacities'. An artillery unit took twenty-four hours to move its guns nine kilometres with losses of 'three dead, nine wounded, twenty-seven with dysentery, twelve with typhus, fifty-seven with severe diarrhoea, and three with frostbite.' Soldiers ate half-cooked meat and cold preserved food if they were lucky. When the artillery unit arrived at its new positions, the men found neither quarters nor food there.

They were also suffering a shortage of rifles. This had reached crisis level: battalions could not be despatched to the front because they did not have rifles. Another shortage was protective clothing. The boots had cardboard soles and the greatcoats contained inferior fibres so they did not keep the cold, damp or wind out. As a result increasing numbers succumbed to frostbite and 'the White Death'. In some units a quarter of casualties simply froze to death. It was so cold the water-cooled machine guns could not be used.

The fighting was hard and the casualties high. Some units were ordered not to take prisoners and there were instances of medical personnel being shot as they attempted to treat the wounded.

On the Austro-Hungarian front, the weather was so bad that no one really knew what was happening except for those freezing to death or dying in order to take a few yards of snow. Sickness was rife. It is estimated that the Austro-Hungarian army lost in the order of 80,0000 men during this campaign.

The large-scale losses increased the demand for replacement troops. As a result men were being transferred where they were needed and not into their normal territorial regiments. The common ethnicity of units became diluted, resulting in a negative effect on morale and cohesiveness. In some cases the replacement officers could not speak the language of the unit they joined. Previous concerns about the reliability of certain ethnic groupings were compounded by the atmosphere of mistrust and disrespect engendered by such random postings. 'In growing numbers, battalions and regiments began deserting en masse to the enemy...Czech deserters now serving in Russian intelligence units encouraged fellow nationals to desert'. Entire battalions surrendered to the Russians in an attempt to escape the freezing conditions when a Russian counter-attack, in the second week of March, terminated Habsburg efforts and put them back where they had started.

They had wanted to save Przemysl but now knew it was not possible. There were no troops available to rescue it. This did not stop Conrad von Hötzendorf trying. Again his troops were bled white by Russian numerical superiority. Again, the weather, frostbite and disease reduced Habsburg numbers so they were unable to pierce the Russian lines. German assistance was not forthcoming. Continued Russian attacks pushed them further back. A lack of field officers did not help the situation, with nearly fifty per cent categorised as missing or lost.

The garrison in Przemysl had realised months back that they had been abandoned when they found that the German troops were staying in Cracow: they were only there to stop a Russian advance into Silesia. The 'cold, bitter winter wreaked havoc on the garrison's morale and its health'. All breakout attempts were unsuccessful and resulted in very heavy loss of life. And no one could get in. By the time the Russian heavy artillery arrived and began to systematically shell the fortifications they were low on food, medicine and ammunition. On 22 March, after nearly 200 days, the garrison capitulated with the loss of 100,000 men.

This released another Russian army for the Carpathians. With the Russians able to send 100,000 troops against the Homonna railroad junction, there was little that the defenders could do. The unrelenting pressure and retreats threatened rear and flank positions. Requests for German help went unheeded as did field commanders' requests for rest time for their men. There were few replacements and the quality of those that were available was much diminished.

While his generals wanted to retreat, Conrad could see no reason to. Thirty-four Habsburg divisions faced twenty-four Russian divisions. What he did not take into account was the greater size of each Russian division. His plan was to halt the Russians with a counter-attack when reinforcing German troops arrived. Conrad's order was simple: "Durchhalten" (Hold out!)

The armies tried, but when they 'surrendered the blood-scarred Manilova heights on 28 March it became questionable whether any of the mauled Habsburg units could maintain their positions for much longer'. Despite commands to hold positions to the point of total sacrifice, whole divisions still retreated, in some cases when there was no pressure from the Russians.

'Commencement of the Carpathian Easter Battle finally halted czarist efforts to break through the tenuous Habsburg positions...The hastily transferred German *Beskiden Corps*...joined the Habsburg *X Corps*...and successfully reversed' the Russians' fortunes. They had paid a high price for their earlier successes and no longer possessed sufficient manpower; their resolve was weakening. They halted, paused and then began preparing for the May offensive. Before then renewed Russian attacks forced further Austrian retreats. While the Russians continued their advance, another problem occurred. It seemed likely that Italy would join the war and force the Habsburgs to fight on three fronts.

With the Russian superiority in guns and numbers of troops, the Austrians continued to fall back. Only the German troops managed to advance. The snows fell again, giving some respite, but the retreats continued. And on 6 April, the Russians began a major offensive.

For days the Russians battered the Habsburg forces causing numerous retreats. However, by the middle of the month they had still not smashed the line and lacked the reinforcements to exploit their advantageous position. Hungary was saved and the stage was set for the early May Gorlice-Tarnow campaign.

By spring 1915, the Germans were also fearful of Italian intervention on the Entente side because Italian attacks would be against the Austrians. The poor performance of the Habsburg forces meant that any decisive victory in Russia needed German troops. For the next offensive German units were inserted into the line.

That new formations were needed resulted from the decision to stay on the defensive in the west and send most of the new formations from the home depots to the east. Eventually over 600,000 German troops would be available for a summer campaign. Although numerically inferior to the Russians in infantry, they were better armed and equipped with an efficient supply service. They also possessed great superiority in heavy artillery and ammunition and their staff were better trained.

'By late April they had concentrated 357,000 Central Powers troops in the Gorlice-Tarnow region against 219,000 Russians. They had also managed to create an advantage in artillery pieces in the sector of 1,500 heavy guns to 700. The Russians never suspected either the size or the intentions of the Central Powers forces opposite them.'

Some of the troops were newly arrived from the west, where they had become accustomed to trench warfare. Here there were mountains and beautiful scenery. One such transfer was Ernst Schallert, a Philosophy student from Berlin. In January, during fighting near Arras he wrote home to report his brother's death and ask them not to grieve. Like many, he was religious and told them to think about two passages from the Gospel of John: 'Greater love hath no man than this, that he lay down his life for his friends' and 'Be thou faithful unto death and I will give thee the crown of life'.

On arrival in Galicia they felt both at home and abroad. In a letter written on his arrival at Hotwina Brzesco, Schallert described what he saw. 'We marched on to the mountains. It was country like our German Mittel-Gebirge: woods of mixed pines, firs and deciduous trees; well-cultivated fields on the slopes. But the inhabitants! The houses! Nothing but wooden hovels in which people and animals live all together with the lice and fleas.' Confident of the success of their future attack and happy with his lot, he told his parents that his 'life has been so beautiful that it may just as well end now' but he had no premonition of his death and that he hoped to survive and work for his ideals. He was to be killed in the fighting near Jaroslav on 24 May.

'The attack opened on 2 May and by the next day General Mackensen, commanding German *Eleventh* and Austrian *Fourth* Armies, had torn a ten-mile gap in the Russian front between Tarnow and Gorlice.'

Soldiers were fighting and dying for different beliefs: some for victory, some for the homeland, some for the excitement, many because they had to. Fritz Philipps, an agricultural student from Jena, was fighting for world peace when killed on the first day of the offensive. He had written his farewell letter to his parents back in October. 'I am going with all my heart, freely and willingly, never doubting but that Germany will bring it to a favourable and victorious end…I need scarcely say that I hate war in itself, but for that very reason I will fight and take part in this great affair and willingly die, if I can thereby contribute to the transformation of World War into World Peace'.

Tarnow fell on 6 May and Jaroslav on 16 May. One soldier who fought in the offensive was Leutnant Count Arthur von Der Groebben. He was an infantry officer in a Guards regiment who had been transferred from France in April. He was looking forward to fighting the Russians and leading his Company into action.

On 8 May, Groebben's unit were to storm Hill 382 at precisely 1000 hours. 'Punctually at 6 in the morning began the hellish concert. The German and Austrian artillery had got the range exactly during the previous days, and shells and shrapnel came roaring over, each with its own peculiar sound – howling, singing, whistling, booming, ear-splittingly crashing – into the Russian position.' From the Russian trenches 'came a continuous rattle of rifle-fire and the regular ticking of machine-guns'. After blowing his whistle three times to launch the assault all he could remember was the 'mad rush forward, wild cheering, screams of fear from the absolutely overwhelmed Russians' and then quiet during which he wrote a report telling his superiors that Hill 382 had been taken with slight casualties and that they were advancing further. Suddenly they had captured Hill 376 and were then far beyond the furthest point of their objective. The Russians were retreating rapidly. Leutnant von Der Groebben was killed in action on 26 May fighting near Jaroslav.

Taking advantage of the German success, the Austrians, further south, advanced steadily throughout the summer. They crossed the Dniester and Bug rivers and captured Przemysl on 3 June, Lemberg on 22 June, Brody on 1 September and Dubno on 7 September.

During the retreat, the Russians torched the villages they passed and in many cases counter-attacked to try to slow the Germans down. Walter Schmidt experienced both during June. He wrote home to describe it: 'Our Midsummer Night was also beautiful, and by way of bonfires the villages all around were blazing. Shrapnel whistled unceasingly, and in the distance we heard faint "hurrahs". The Russians were making a counter-attack in honour of St. John's Night, and were so absolutely wiped out that in the morning each of our Companies discovered 200 dead Russians.'

The Russian retreat created a deep salient in Poland that was vulnerable to German encirclement. Hindenburg wanted to close the salient with an attack from Vilna in the north and Tarnopol in the south but the Chief of the General Staff had a more limited view. The attack was to be limited to linking up at Brest-Litovsk.

In early July, *Fourth, Eleventh* and *Bug Armies* turned north and on 13 July, *Ninth* and *Twelfth Armies* attacked towards Warsaw. On 25 July the Narew river was crossed by *Twelfth Army* and on 5 August *Ninth Army* entered Warsaw. In the south, the combined Austro-German drive, between the Bug and Vistula took Lublin and Kholm on 30 and 31 July. 'By mid-August the two Austro-German pincers had joined near Brest-Litovsk and the city itself was taken on the 25th. *Bug Army* went on to take Pinsk on 16 September but the Russians, despite heavy casualties, had once again managed to elude a strategic encirclement.'

Even with the Russians in retreat, many realised that the end was not near. 'Fancy still dwelling on the thought of being at home again! We have been disappointed so often! First we hoped to be back by the end of October, 1914; then by Christmas; then Easter; then Christmas, 1915; and now we are forced to admit that it can't be over before Easter, 1916.' For the writer, Walter Schmidt, a student of Natural History at Tübingen University, the war would end on 16 April, 1917, when he was killed in action near Laon in France after two years' service in Russia.

North of the Bug, three German armies (*Eighth, Tenth and Twelfth*) moved eastwards. Between 17 August and 2 September they had captured Bialystok, Grodno and Kovno. One casualty of the September fighting was Eduard Bruhn, a student from Kiel who wrote his last letter home on 17 September, the day he died:

Dear Parents,

I am lying on the battle-field badly wounded. Whether I recover is in God's hands. If I die, do not weep. I am going blissfully home. A hearty greeting to you all once more. May God soon send you peace and grant me a blessed home-coming. Jesus is with me, so it is easy to die. In heartfelt love,

Eduard.

When the fighting stopped, men had time to grieve for their friends and wonder what would become of them, knowing that death could appear at any time. During a break in the fighting near the River Serwetsch, Sergeant Beck, a law student from Leipzig went looking in the divisional cemetery for his friend from home. The inscription read, Sergeant Wilde, August 10, 1915. Standing by the grave his thoughts went back to a time before they had left for the war. 'Another young life cut short. Thirty years only…I still remember the last days in Strahlsund when we were with his little fiancée and all so merry'. Back with his men that evening, there is no shooting. The quiet is broken only by a harmonica playing waltz-tunes in a melancholy way. Four new soldiers join the company during the quiet. Within two hours one of them is dead, killed by a stray bullet.

'In the far north, from 15 July, *Niemen Army* advanced up the coast to Libau, taken a few days later, and then turned eastwards towards Mitau and Riga. The former fell on 1 August but the drive to Riga then stalled, with an attempted supporting landing at Pernau, on 17 August, being an ignominious failure.'

Despite this setback, *Niemen Army* continued its advance towards Dvinsk and the River Drina. After Kovno fell on 17 August, the advance slowed and, apart from a substantial cavalry probe towards Minsk, it halted in early September. Vilna did not fall until 18 September and the cavalry were repulsed south of Dvinsk. Another attempted encirclement failed and the Russians managed to extricate the major part of the two trapped armies. By the end of the month, the whole Eastern Front was static. In terms of losses the German campaign had been a strategic victory, but to Ludendorff its success was only tactical.

The new Russian line ran from just south of Riga down to Czernowitz in the Bukovina. Although their army had not fallen as far back as Kiev, the Austro-German forces were well inside Russia. Major-General Hoffmann regarded the Russians as having been beaten along the whole front but not so convincingly 'as to compel them to sue for peace'. 'With the Russians pushed back, the Austrians and Germans proceeded to the next stage of Falkenhayn's grand strategy: the final subjugation of Serbia.' On 11 October, Bulgaria joined the Central Powers.

While the Russian Army had been retreating, the French asked when the Russians could mount their next offensive. They were told December.

On 23 December, 500,000 men from three armies assaulted the German *South* and the Austrian *Seventh Armies*. The Russian assault was a feint. Its purpose was to draw German reserves south of Czernowitz while the main attack was driven towards Bessarabia.

After a thirty-six hour bombardment, the Russians attacked. Alerted by aerial reconnaissance, the Austrians repulsed repeated attacks, inflicting heavy losses.

Further north there was still time for Christmas. Hans Stegemann, a forestry student, wrote home to describe the beauty of the woods nearby and danger in his life. 'I am having such a good time here just now that I never want to move!...On Christmas Eve...I was sitting in a most picturesque corner of this incomparable wooded country, with my pipe in my mouth...It was an unforgettably beautiful evening'. Going on his rounds with Corporal Haupt, they tested the strength of the ice on the river and were shot at because they had forgotten their snow clothing. Haupt was wounded so they crawled back to the NCOs quarters where a sleigh was phoned for to take Haupt to an aid post. Continuing his rounds from post to post, he found 'every one had a little lit-up Christmas tree,' with plenty of 'Love-gifts' from home. His own Christmas started at 2200 hours in his block-house when all the senior NCOs and his company commander joined him. 'A lot of champagne had been sent up and it was very cheery. Best of all was the lovely little Christmas tree which my batman had decorated. We sang Christmas carols to mouth-organ accompaniment, and everything was just as it ought to be at Christmas.' Even the Russians did not disturb them.

On the last day of 1915, another heavy bombardment rained down on the Austrian positions. In the succeeding assault the Habsburgs were driven back about a quarter of a mile on a thousand yard front at Rarance. 'No further infantry attacks were attempted, but an intermittent artillery duel lasted for another two weeks until, in mid-January, Ivanov (Commander of the Southwestern Front), reluctant to waste ammunition or risk further lives, decided to let the battle die down.'

Although there had been this year-end attack, in which the Austrians had been pushed back, at the end of the year overall it seemed to the German High Command that 'the Russians were at the end of their rope. They had been chased from Poland, had suffered repeated massive defeats and had shown their system of war was wholly unsuited to the modern, industrial battlefields of 1914 and 1915. Russian generalship had ranged from the uninspiring to the abysmal, and the Russian transport and economic systems were already showing serious signs of cracking. Despite their ability to retreat into their own massive territory and call upon seemingly endless manpower reserves, Russia appeared to most Germans as a fatally wounded nation whose last death throes could not possibly be far away.'

'For the Central Powers, 1915 was the best year of the war. Despite commitments to several fronts, the Germans had frustrated repeated Allied offensives in the west. To the east, the Germans had achieved a spectacular breakthrough in Poland and bolstered the armies of their Austrian Ally. In the southeast, their Turkish Allies had thwarted an Allied effort to turn the strategic flank with an invasion of the Dardanelles peninsula. In the fall came more good news, when Bulgaria entered the war on the side of Central Powers.' The Serbs were finally beaten, allowing an overland link to the Middle East.

While the developments of the year offered immediate grounds for some optimism, the long-term implications were less encouraging. Triumph in the east and stalemate in the west had been repeated with no sign of the end of the war. 'The strain on German resources mounted as the conflict broadened.' Germany's commitment to fighting in Africa, Asia Minor, Belgium, Poland, Russia, Serbia and the Tyrol depleted resources. The strategic dilemma was not easily solved. The east needed more troops but the west took priority. With the Russian ability to bear tremendous losses, most German commanders believed it could not be won on the east. However, conditions in the west 'frustrated the kind of offensive action that victory seemed to require'. While many were questioning Falkenhayn's thinking, the decision was made for Verdun.

A posed photo of German troops leaving their trench at the start of an attack.

Law and order were very strict under the Habsburgs in newly occupied territory. Even minor infractions could lead to the death penalty in order to 'encourage the others'. Those with anti-Habsburg feelings were summarily executed.

It was not just civilians who felt Habsburg justice. Here soldiers and civilians have been executed.

Sometimes a placard was hung round the victim's neck as a warning to what would happen to others.

Here a leading citizen is publicly hanged, with a large audience, as an example to make people co-operate with the victors.

Franz Wengbauer, an Austro-Hungarian soldier who died on 16 December 1915, in a **POW** hospital at Nikolsk in Russia.

27. April 1915.

UnterJäger (corporal) Anton Huber died in an Hungarian epidemic hospital on 23 February 1915. He was forty when he died and had been serving with *4 Platoon, 4 Company of FeldJäger Battalion 8.*

Birthday menu card for General Hans Hartwig von Beseler, the victor of Antwerp. Shortly before his birthday he was transferred to the Eastern Front where he was subordinated to General von Gallwitz's *Guard Reserve Corps.* In August, after his victory at Novogeorgievsk, he became Governor-general of *Generalgouvernement Warschau,* the zone of Polish lands under German military rule.

Polish peasants being guarded by front-line German infantry.

An Austrian trench somewhere in Galicia. To prevent the collapse of the sides it is revetted with thin branches.

Twenty-year-old Infanterist Brunner was serving in *7 Company* of *18 Reserve Infantry Regiment,* when he was killed in action on 17 August 1915. His regiment was part of *1 Reserve Infantry Division* and had fought on the Eastern Front since the start of the war. At the time of his death the regiment was in Kurland.

Franz Hofmann was wounded during the Gorlice-Tarnów offensive and died of his wounds in a Duisburg hospital. He was a reservist serving in *9 Company* of *12 Reserve Infantry Regiment,* in *5 Reserve Division.*

Raimund Pöll went to the Eastern Front in January 1915 and joined *K.u.K. Infantry Regiment 49.* He was killed in action on 24 June.

An Austrian Jäger Company pose during a lull in the summer fighting in the Carpathians.

Josef Birnbeck from Rosenheim in Bavaria, was a war volunteer. He was serving in *7 Company* of *249 Infantry Regiment*, when at the age of eighteen-and-a-half he was killed in action in Russia on 7 August 1915.

A Christmas 1915 keepsake. Austrian and German POWs pose for their photo somewhere in Siberia.

A youthful 1915 Habsburg soldier wearing the standard uniform: pike grey field service cap, winter field jacket, 1915 knee trousers and puttees.

Funeral service for two recently deceased soldiers somewhere in Poland. Judging by the age of most of the men, this is a Landwehr unit.

A poor quality coloured photo of Austrian artillery in the Carpathians. It clearly shows the dramatic landscape the battles took place in.

Right: Horse-drawn transport fording a small river in the Carpathians.

Below: Snipers were found everywhere and the unwary paid the price. Here German soldiers try and find the direction of the shot while their own sniper waits patiently.

Above: Radio had become an essential part of modern warfare. When used carefully it was very useful, but when used 'en clair' the other side could find out what their enemy was doing. To improve speed, Russian orders were sometimes sent without the use of code and even those in code were usually quickly cracked, providing much useful intelligence.

The machine gun ruled the battlefield. This is heavy 08 Maxim with full shield.

Letters and parcels from home helped maintain morale and gave soldiers something to look forward to. Newly arrived mail was sorted and then taken to the unit. For some unexplained reason some of it needed kicking before sorting. A trooper of *6 Chevauleger Regiment* in the *Bavarian Cavalry Division* sent this card.

An unknown
German soldier
who had his photo
taken on Friday 21
May 1915 in
Russian Poland.

Christmas 1915 in the Carpathians. Members of *Hoch und Deutschmeister Regiment Nr. 4* pose for a photo to send home to their families in Vienna.

A lightly protected village in Poland. Ryki was obviously of little importance or, when the photo was taken, was far behind the line. There is minimal wire and a moveable barricade to stop any attack.

A postcard produced to raise funds to help East Prussian refugees. Three German soldiers taking dinner back to the trenches from a Polish market.

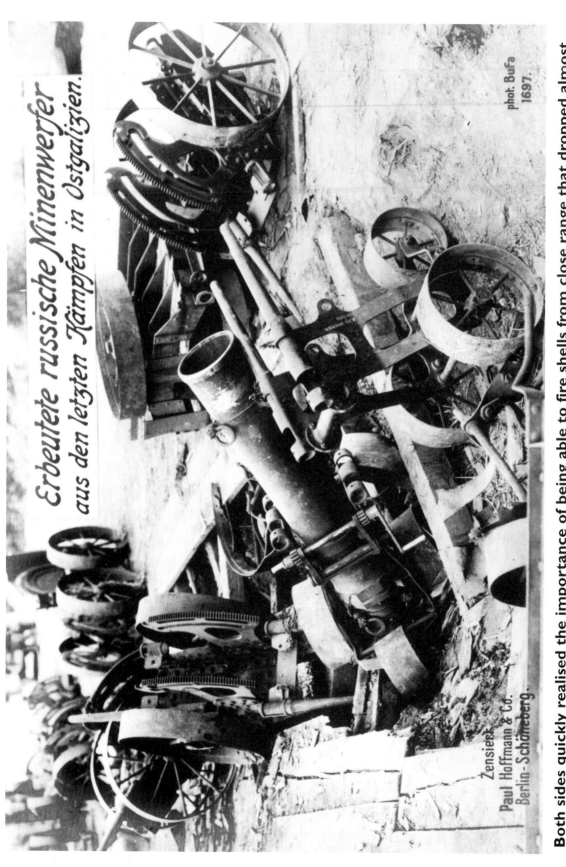

Erbeutete russische Minenwerfer aus den letzten Kämpfen in Ostgalizien.

phot. BuFa
1697.

Zensiert.
Paul Hoffmann & Co.
Berlin-Schöneberg.

Both sides quickly realised the importance of being able to fire shells from close range that dropped almost vertically into the enemy's trench. These are Russian trench mortars captured in the last fight in East Galicia. The mortar's chief advantage was that it could be fired from the (relative) safety of the trench, avoiding exposure of the mortar crews to the enemy. It was also notably lighter and more mobile than other artillery pieces.

'On the march to battle'. German infantry pass through a ruined Polish town on their way to the front during the winter of 1915.

An Austrian mobile field cooker, a goulash cannon, set-up in a deserted Russian village. Warm food was essential to keep up morale, and the men's strength, but during bad weather it frequently failed to get to the front line; men often fought for days without food of any description.

Der Krieg im Osten
Deutsche Kolonisation im Osten — Eingang zur Kolonie

One German war aim was to release land in the east for German settlers. This card, by an East Prussian photographer, is entitled: The war in the east. German colonization in the east - entrance to the colony.

Clerical work was essential no matter where the army went, in this case Brest-Litovsk during October 1915. The photo was sent by a soldier in one of the *Bug Army's* Lorry Parks to his girlfriend in Wald in North Rhine-Westphalia.

A group of decorated officers and NCOs standing outside a typical Russian house. The boy is probably a servant.

NCOs relaxing in Russia during July 1915.

'From the Eastern Theatre of War' – A medical shelter with Assmann beds.

German artillerists in front of their covered field gun. The stacked rifles are M88 carbines, an obsolete model using 8mm ammunition that was issued to rear echelon troops, unlikely to have to use it.

An unknown soldier posing for his family back in Beeskow near Berlin. He was serving with *6 Reserve Division* and had been fighting in the Gorlice-Tarnów offensive when this photo was taken.

Oldenburg Landwehr troups in Russia, September 1915.

The Landsturm Narew Bridge watch detachment in the ruins of Ostrolenka in 1915. Note the range of uniforms for a December day.

Prince Leopold of Bavaria awarding Bavarian soldiers with the Iron Cross. On 16 April 1915, he was given command of *9 Army*, replacing General Mackensen. Leopold was an able commander taking Warsaw on 4 August 1915. Following this, he was given command of Army Group Prince Leopold of Bavaria (*Heeresgruppe Prinz Leopold von Bayern*), which was a combined German/Austro-Hungarian force in the central sector of the Eastern Front. On 29 August 1916, he became the Supreme Commander of the German forces on the Eastern front (*Oberbefehlshaber Ost*), succeeding Hindenburg, a post he held for the rest of the war.

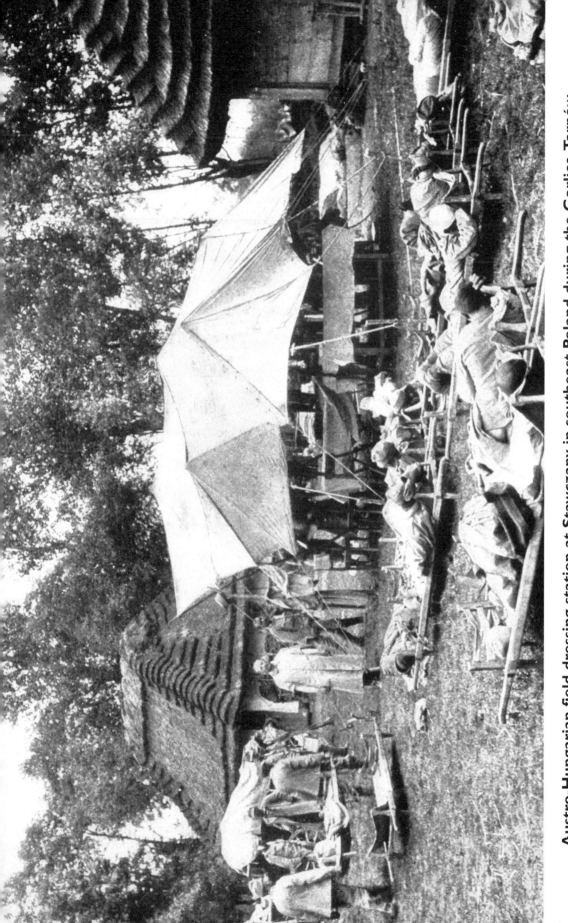

Austro-Hungarian field dressing station at Stawczany in southeast Poland during the Gorlice-Tarnów offensive. In the centre is a doctor/medical orderly with both hands covered in blood. To provide a sheltered area, groundsheets have been joined together to make canopy.

Chapter 3
1916
Helping the Western Front

'Over Christmas 1915, Falkenhayn had submitted a memorandum on the state of the war and prospects for the coming year to the scrutiny of his All-Highest War-Lord. He was opposed to further offensive action on the blank plains of Russia.' Falkenhayn expected the Russian state's problems to cause it to collapse in the near future but Hindenburg was not so complacent. He knew the German extended line was inadequately held and needed more troops.

Pointing to the summer successes, Falkenhayn told Hindenburg and Ludendorff there would be no major initiatives on their front. He also denied them any reinforcements and withdrew all German troops from Galicia, leaving its defence to the Austrians who were more occupied 'with defeating Serbia and planning an offensive against Italy'. For Falkenhayn the west was where the war could be won: Verdun was chosen as the place to bleed France to death. Stavka chose to break this complacency with a major attack in March.

Winter passed with only minor activity by both sides on the Northern Front. Each army now dug-in to strengthen their positions. The German trenches were 'strongly built in concrete, equipped with light railways and often their own generating plants, they included bomb-proof shelters. Recreation areas had been established not far behind the lines'. On the other side of the wire, the Russians were producing trenches that were comfortable. Walls were planked and stoves provided heating. There were even opportunities for relaxation.

The object of the three-pronged Russian attack was to throw the German northern wing back to the Baltic coast. When the build-up of forces had been completed, the Russians were to have numerical manpower superiority of 5:1 supported by artillery on an unprecedented scale. Captured soldiers in peasant dress and observed troop concentrations led the Germans to conclude an attack was likely.

The spring thaw began the day before the start of the offensive. After an eight-hour bombardment, the Russians launched their attack. Everywhere it failed. The next day the attack was resumed and although the situation was critical at times the German lines held: 'the barbed wire in front of the German trenches was hung with the corpses of Russian attackers as far as the eye could see'. The same happened the next day, but when winter returned during the night the Russians were able to advance through relatively unprotected swamps. Little progress was made on day five until early evening when the Germans were threatened with disaster.

As the temperature rose, so did the water level. Everywhere turned to mud. Leutnant Stegemann wrote home describing the sudden change in his sector on the Dvina. 'The river suddenly rose during the night of April 2nd with overwhelming force and rapidity. The previous afternoon the water in the flooded meadows had already risen so considerably that I had to send rations to posts about a mile away…in a boat'. The men in the boat were caught in the flood and its accompanying ice floes. 'The water rose five feet in an hour. The floating masses of ice…capsized the boat'. In the pitch-dark night his men had to vacate 'seven block-houses in a twinkling'. His own dug-out disappeared under the water.

The men held onto the capsized boat while efforts were made to establish telephonic contact with troops in the rear. Eventually a boat was found but all the time the water was rising, making it more difficult to get to the men. Then it was realised that thirty men were trapped in houses near the river bank; fortunately a bigger boat had been called for as well. Frozen and done in, all Stegemann could do was wait. While doing so, he changed his clothes, and smoked a cigar while drinking five glasses of brandy in an attempt to warm himself up.

During the wait, the boat from the rear area had managed to pick up three of the men in the river. Frozen through, they were sent off to hospital. By first light all his men had been rescued, except a sixteen-year-old corporal whose body was never recovered. His company now had new positions overlooking a two-mile broad lake. Other units were not as lucky as Stegemann's: many men were drowned by the flood.

The rising water level and the mud made movement difficult and the dense fogs caused units to lose contact. As the front turned into a lake, the Russians called off their attacks and withdrew troops. Any Russian success was short-lived. On 28 April, after a high explosive barrage followed by gas, against which the Russians were unprotected, the German infantry reclaimed their lost positions in just one day.

Much concern had been expressed about the loyalty of some of the ethnic groups that made up the Habsburg forces. While there was no concern over German troops deserting, many of the ethnic groups in the Russian Army were happy to cross over to the Germans. Oskar Greulich was serving near Świniuchy during the April thaw. As on the Western Front, there was some degree of live-and-let-live in the east and religious festivals were often observed. 'For some time not a shot has been fired on either side, although everybody is calmly walking about on the top, and even taking an afternoon nap up there!'

Whilst wary, both sides felt it foolish to disturb each other by shooting. 'When the Russian sentry goes on duty, he thinks it necessary to inform his vis-à-vis of the fact. "Morning, Auyoosht!" he calls across the lake.' Initially they did not respond or just sent an occasional bullet across, which was met by cries of 'Germanski damn! Shoot nix!' Greulich and his men then realised that their opponents were Lithuanians and Poles:' It is a good thing that there is a lake between us,' he wrote, 'otherwise many of these men would certainly have deserted to us.'

Both sides were religious, especially Bavarian soldiers. 'On Easter Eve they (the Russians) called out:"Germanski shoot nix. Tomorrow peace!"' The Russians then treated the Germans to a concert with mandolins and violins, 'as beautiful as any one could hear at Easter in Eichelburg. In the evening the male voice choir strikes up, and solemn chants – no doubt Easter hymns – ring out into the night in three parts and sung by very good voices.'

Across the front many units witnessed similar events but only in the front line. In the rear, headquarters staff kept on planning. At the Austrian HQ, the Italian problem was paramount. They were not expecting a Russian offensive, had become obsessed with Italy, and had dedicated most of their staff energies to planning a south Tyrol offensive. To give the offensive every chance of success, they moved six infantry divisions from Galicia. Unknown to them, Brusilov had four armies, ready to strike consecutive blows along a nineteen-mile front. Careful shepherding of reserves had given the Russians a superiority of 125,000 men. Fortunately for the Russians, their postponed attack coincided with the birthday of the *Fourth Army* commander, so many key officers were not in place when the attack came.

The offensive began on 4 June with a hurricane bombardment (using two weeks' supply of ammunition) that destroyed, except for some deep bunkers, the first three lines of the Austrian positions in Galicia. Part of the success was due to the Russian use of aircraft equipped with radio to direct the gunfire accurately. 'The barrage continued throughout the day and well into the night to prevent the enemy repairing his barbed wire under cover of darkness, but was temporarily halted between midnight and 2.30 a.m. so that scouts could inspect the damage.'

The Austrian *Fourth Army* front collapsed. Against minimal resistance, the Russians were able to push a wedge between *Fourth Army* and *Böhm-Ermolli's Army Group*. By the following day 40,000 prisoners had been taken, a number that swelled as the offensive spread along the line.

As *Fourth Army* collapsed, its neighbour, *Seventh Army*, retreated south. In turn *First Army* withdrew, putting the whole Austro-Hungarian position in considerable danger. Whole units melted away with some joining the Russian forces. 'By the third day of the offensive, the severity of the situation was plain for all to see. The Russians had torn open a sizeable hole 32Km (20 miles) wide in the Austro-Hungarian front. Hundreds of thousands of Austro-Hungarian troops were prisoners of war or had simply fled from the battlefield.'

After four days of fighting *Fourth Army* had shrunk from 110,000 to just 18,000 men under arms. As many as sixty per cent of the casualties were actually deserters.

'Only in the centre was there little progress. Here Sakharov's Eleventh (Army) had met Bothmer's German-Austrian *South Army* which repulsed all assaults upon it.' However, even here there was success. On 15 July, warned by his intelligence about a forthcoming attack on 18 July by *Südarmee*, Sakharov launched his own pre-emptive assault which took 1,300 prisoners and captured much of the ammunition stockpiled for the German attack.

Even though some Russian commanders did not attack until the due date and the northern end of the South West Front was pinned down, the advance moved rapidly. 'By 17 June Czernowitz was taken and, on the 21st, the entire province of Bukovina. By the 23rd, the Russians were in Kimpolung and once more threatened the Carpathian foothills.'

Austro-Hungarian units were in retreat on a 250 mile front from the Pripet marshes to the Carpathians. German help would be forthcoming but only with strings. The South Tyrol campaign was to be closed, and troops moved from that front to Russia were to be under German control.

However, the Russians did not have it all their own way. Falkenhayn was concerned about the Lutsk salient and managed to build up an eight division force (mixed Austrian and German units), without much opposition from the Russians. Commanded by General von der Marwitz, the force struck in the Kovel area. In four days of fierce fighting, they recovered a few miles of ground.

The Russian gains so far included 350,000 Austrian prisoners, 400 artillery pieces and 1,300 machine guns. Many defenders had been killed and wounded along a 200 mile-long front that had been penetrated, in places, to a depth of forty miles. On the Russian side, losses had also been heavy with over 300,000 casualties. Ammunition for the artillery was also very short. A great deal had been achieved by an offensive designed to pin down forces before the principal attack.

Brusilov's men rested and waited for their supply columns. Without support from other armies the offensive would stall. None came, and, while the Russian commanders fought among themselves, the Germans moved four divisions from France and five from East Front reserves. The Austro-Hungarians also moved four divisions from the South Tyrol Front and the Turks sent troops to help.

No second Russian attack materialised. This gave the Germans time 'to set up solid defensive lines, restore discipline and assume command of Austro-Hungarian units as small as companies'. The control by the German Army was confirmed when on 27 July, Hindenburg was made Supreme Commander of the Eastern Front with control of all military operations in the east. This was followed by the Kaiser becoming titular head of the United Supreme Command. The Habsburg army now had little say in its role.

The appointment of Hindenburg gave rise to great rejoicing among many of the troops, mainly because he had never lost a battle. Leutnant Stegemann described the men's reactions: 'I was quite astonished at my Hanseatickers, Mechlinburgers and Holsteiners, they were so wild with joy at the news.' He was now the Company Commander and enjoying the responsibility.

Ordered to renew the offensive, Brusilov's forces attacked on 27 July, routing the remnants of the Austro-Hungarian First Army. A pivotal point between Brusilov and Evert's fronts was Kovel. With the offensive losing impetus, its capture became very important. The Tsar, as commander-in-chief, decided that this task should be undertaken by his Guards Army. The plan was for the infantry to break through and the cavalry to attack, routing the Germans. The attack was launched without artillery support and with insufficient preparation: the troops had to cut through the barbed wire before they could move. On the left the Russians were successful, taking 11,000 prisoners, forty-six guns and sixty-five machine guns, but losses were heavy.

They were especially heavy in some units of First Corps, whose commander felt that a flank attack was beneath his troops. He sent two of the finest Russian Regiments – the Preobrazhensky Guards and the Imperial Rifle Regiment – in a frontal attack along a causeway. Casualties were so heavy 'many preferred to wade waist-deep through the bog' even though their slow progress made them excellent targets for the German machine gunners and for the planes that bombed them. To make matters worse, their commander had forgotten to tell the artillery of the changed plan so they were shelled by their own side. With seventy per cent casualties, they took their objective, but the supporting cavalry withdrew and they were forced to abandon their gains.

A further attempt to take Kovel, as part of the re-opened offensive, appeared to be achieving results. Then the flanks failed and the impossible happened – the Guards withdrew. The reason was clear the next day. An army, classed by Major-General Knox as "'physically the finest human animals in Europe" had lost 55,000 men. Throughout the army and the country there was an almost speechless fury at the whole catastrophic and futile episode'.

The advance continued. On 28 July Brody fell, Monstryska was occupied on 7 August, Nadworna fell on 12 August. Russian troops were across *Südarmee's* lines of communication. There was no option but to pull back to the Zlota Lipa line to defend Lemberg.

As the offensive moved forward, it met German units that offered stiffer resistance. The advance slowed down and became costlier. Other fronts were stripped of men and equipment to keep up the pressure but this created bottlenecks and funnelled troops into positions where the Germans were at their strongest. Despite desperate attacks in August and September, the front eventually solidified.

It had been a bad period for the Central Powers. Between 4 June and mid-August, they had lost 400,000 men as prisoners and 15,000 square miles of territory. Their total losses were probably around 750,000 men. But many Russians had also been taken prisoner, sometimes gladly, as Adolf Stürmer, a law student who had volunteered in 1914, found out. He had volunteered for a patrol that was to blow up a bridge to slow down the Russian advance. Crossing the river they surprised a Russian post. There was no fight. The biggest Russian, immediately 'made the sign of the cross and then put up his hands. Then they were all full of joy; kissed our hands and coats; tore the cockades out of their caps, and threw down their arms'.

It was a decisive victory, arguably the greatest achievement of the war but it had been won at a high cost. 'Brusilov's losses were 450,000 and his reserves reduced from 400,000 to 100,000. Total Russian war losses were now 5½ million. It had been a spectacular but Pyrrhic victory that weakened and destabilised the Romanov Empire, and gained little of strategic importance.' All eyes then turned to Romania.

Romania's entry into the war meant that Brusilov had to make a fresh effort in support of Russia's new ally. On 29 August, Bothmer's *Südarmee* was attacked at Brzezany and the town of Potutory taken. While the offensive failed in its main purpose of removing a German salient because of stubborn German resistance, Niziov on the Dniester fell and the Austrians were forced back to Halicz. Continued fighting brought the Russians some local successes, but the continual reinforcement of Bothmer's men meant that there was no chance of a serious Russian success. And with the Romanians quickly needing help, the Russian focus moved further south.

The Romanian retreat after their defeat at Kronstadt meant a further change in Russian plans. Although twenty-seven Russian divisions moved to help, a further Romanian retreat meant that the Russian front had to be extended 400 kilometres. This new responsibility was paid for at the expense of Brusilov's offensive.

Russian officers blamed the Romanians for their situation, but in truth, their offensive effort had been slacking because of a shortage of men and arms. They were now fighting against positions where reinforcements could be made available. The balance of strength had also shifted. 'At the beginning of the battle 39 Russian infantry divisions opposed 37 Austrian and one German division. By 12 August, reinforcements from other fronts had increased the South West Front to 61, but they were opposed by 72 enemy divisions of which 24 were German – 18 having been sent from the west.'

Writing home on 3 September, Leutnant Stegemann described the fighting his company had been through. 'Fierce but victorious battles. I have been through some ghastly times. On the 31st August the Company lost three officers and 50 men, mostly in hand-to-hand fighting…The Russians attack every day, but are always repulsed with terrific loss'. Three days later he was awarded the Iron Cross First Class by Excellenz Litzmann, Hindenburg's second-in-command and a Stegemann family friend. Litzmann sent his greetings to the family and told him to 'write this: I congratulate you on the success of your son, who, through his smartness and courage, with the assistance of his splendid Company, has by his counter-attacks driven back the already demoralized Russians, and by storming Hill 259 averted what was a grave menace to my army-group.' Two weeks later he was killed in action. General Litzmann wrote to his parents when he heard the news. 'I wish to express my deep sympathy with you and your wife. You may both feel proud of your son, and may say to yourselves that you have offered up a sacrifice to the Fatherland the influence of which will be of lasting value to the brave 165th Regiment. Our heroes do not die in vain and they live on for us through their shining example. Leutnant Stegemann, who held the recaptured Hill 259 for 5½ hours against overwhelming odds with the greatest gallantry, and only after the last cartridge had been fired fought his way, with his little handful of men, back through the Russian ranks, will never be forgotten.'

Brusilov had been ordered to stop the attacks but insisted on a few days longer. On 16 17 October fifteen divisions attacked towards Vladimir-Volhynskyi and its railway lines. German artillery caused heavy casualties among the attacking troops but without spotter planes the Russian artillery could do nothing to affect the outcome. After two days the Russians abandoned the battle. The last campaign of the Russian Army had been mounted on behalf of Italy and, the Russians believed, destroyed by Romania.

In Russia there were food and fuel shortages. The number of strikes was increasing and the dissatisfaction was spreading to the armed forces. Military rioters were shot as were soldiers who fired on the police during a strike at the Renault factory in Petrograd. There was discontent in the navy and merchant marine: during 1915 there had been mutinies aboard two ships. 'Amidst these manifestations of unrest, the government remained paralysed by internal upheaval.'

Some realised that 'the long-awaited revolution was moving closer' and began to plan their programmes for when it arrived. Only one of the many plots and conspiracies hatched in the last month of the year came to fruition: Rasputin, a court favourite and confidant of the Tsarina, was murdered by a trio that included a Prince. One of his predictions would come true before the war ended. 'If he died at the hands of any member of the royal family the dynasty would fall within a year, and that its principal members would suffer violent deaths.'

However, the discontent was in the rear. At the front the troops were outwardly untouched. Reinforcements had arrived and morale was good. Heavy artillery was arriving from Britain and supplies were at a high level, putting them on a parity with the Germans. Although fraternisation was not allowed, from the messages exchanged by both sides it was clear that the Austro-Germans were war-weary. The British naval blockade was working and they were hungry: at times they crossed the lines to beg for food from the Russians. They were also aware of the growing Russian strength, realised that there was no breakdown of authority among the front-line soldiers, and knew that they could not leave the Habsburgs to look after the front themselves.

A posed photo showing an Austro-Hungarian bombing party cutting its way through enemy wire. The soldier on the right has wire cutters and, like the others, is carrying grenades in his belt. They are carrying the Steyr-Mannlicher M1895 rifle, nicknamed the "Ruck-Zuck" ("right now" or "very quick").

Something to enjoy: parcels from home.

Medical staff enjoying a meal by their ambulance at the field hospital near Kowel in Poland.

An attempt to organise a local truce so that the wounded can be brought in and the dead removed for burial. Trumpets were used to signal the Russians before the flag was raised.

The residence of the Metropolitans of Bukovina that was used by the Austrians as a field hospital. It was also the Franz-Josefs Universität, founded in 1875. The building was designed by Josef Hlavka and was awarded Deuxieme Prix - Second Grand Prix - at the 1867 World Exhibition in Paris. It is now a World Heritage site.

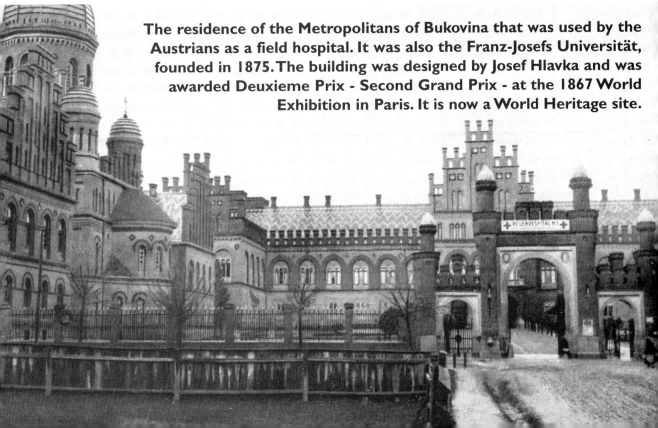

Revetted Austrian trenches with firing point built into the side. Note the lack of wire compared to the Western Front.

An Austro-Hungarian heavy artillery gun being loaded. It is situated in a wood to disguise its firing position.

A German map of the southern sector of the Russian front to show gains between December 1915 and January 1916.

Relaxing in the sun in a Russian forest: reading, playing cards or just watching. Many of them are wearing protective face nets to stop the many biting insects.

Guard duty in an extremely quiet part of the front. The soldier is watching from behind the wire and is making no effort to hide himself. Empty cans have been hung on the wire to act as alarms should Russians try and move through the wire during the night.

Compared to the British and French, the German Army used considerably more horses thereby creating problems with foodstuff. Here troops are crossing a deep rivulet using rather emaciated horses.

Pioneers crossing the Narotsch River in Belarussia. German army pioneers were regarded as a separate combat arm trained in construction and demolition of fortifications, but they were often used as emergency infantry. One battalion was assigned to each Corps.

Drainage work and trench digging were hard, backbreaking jobs on all fronts.

Ambulance convoy in the winter of 1915 travelling towards the Duna (Dvina), a river that drains into the Gulf of Riga in the Baltic.

Deep snow made movement very difficult for wheeled vehicles so the Germans copied the local method of transport, the sledge, pulled by men or horses. Before the snow became too deep, it was possible to clear the road using a horse-pulled snowplough.

A posed photo to show how well the wounded were treated. Landwehr men wait to take the stretcher away while the wounded soldier is dealt with. The soldier on the right is wearing a bayonet troddel (knot), quickly removed by front line troops but often worn by rear echelon troops.

Breakfast in the trenches.

After Stand To! in the morning, breakfast and essential jobs, there was little to do but rest. Here there are supplies waiting to be moved but clearly not during the midday sun.

A German baggage column advancing past a forest in Russia accompanied by marching Infantry.

A home in the dunes. Jägers returning to their billet in the dunes after patrolling along the Baltic coast.

A church service at Stryy in the Ukraine for civilians and military personnel.

A grenadier regiment marching past the Kaiser who is standing on a specially constructed platform.

Südarmee High Command at lunch. That this army consisted of Austrian and German units is clearly shown by the uniforms being worn.

15cm Austrian howitzers near Tudynka getting ready to fire.

The unsanitary and squalid conditions that many of the Poles and Russians lived in spread unwanted guests and diseases. One attempt to halt the spread of Epidemic Typhus and Trench Fever was the delousing station. During the Great War typhus caused three million deaths in Russia and more in Poland. Delousing stations were established for troops on the Western front and to a more limited extent on the east for German troops, but the disease ravaged the armies of the Eastern front. Fatalities were generally between 10 to 40 per cent of those infected, and the disease was a major cause of death for those nursing the sick.

A captured Russian barbed wire dump.

Ungefährer Verlauf des nördl. Teiles der **Ostfront**, die im Jahre 1916 nicht wesentl. geändert wurde

A German map of the northern part of the Russian front in 1916.

General von Pflanzer-Baltin with his staff. In the autumn of 1914, when Romania appeared to be turning against the Central Powers, he was charged with the defence of Transylvania. When the Russians crossed the Carpathians, and there was immediate danger of their driving onto the plains of Hungary, Pflanzer-Baltin, with an improvised division conducted a defence by taking the offensive. After fighting with varying success in the southern part of Eastern Galicia and in the Bukovina, the *VII. Army* under his command, was driven back by the Brusilov offensive in June 1916, and he was relieved of his command.

Generaloberst von Tersztyansky. On the 7th of June 1916 he took over command of the Austrian *4th Army*. He was to support General Marwitz's Armeegruppe during the new counter-attack at the end of June 1916. During this new offensive, *4th Army* received very heavy casualties and was not able to reach the objective of Luck. In July and August 1916, his army found itself in a very critical situation during the Russian counter-attacks at Luck and Kowel, again sustaining very heavy casualties. After receiving new troops, *4th Army* performed reasonably during the autumn Russian offensive especially at Kortytnia, Swincky and Zaturcy before the fighting wound down due to exhaustion on both sides.

Erzhog Karl Franz Joseph, Prinz Leopold von Bavaria (centre, turning away) and General von Woyrsch. Von Woyrsch had retired in 1911 but returned to duty in August 1914 to command the *Landwehr Corps*. He was quickly sent to help the Austro-Hungarian Army fighting in Poland. His troops came up to the Vistula and reinforced the left wing of the Habsburg army under General von Krasnik. In the three-day battle, Woyrsch covered the retreat of the Austrians with his corps *Landwehrkanal*. In July 1915 Woyrsch was involved in the breakthrough battle of Sienno near Wongrowitz (Wągrowiec), and in 1916 he helped fight off the Brusilov Offensive. He was promoted Generalfeldmarschall in 1917.

General Ludendorff with OberstLeutnant Hoffmann, a military strategist widely regarded as one of the finest staff officers of the imperial period.

Christmas 1916 behind the lines in a nice comfortable billet.

Der König von Bayern an der Ostfront auf einem Weichseldampfer.

Zensiert
Paul Hoffmann & Co.
Berlin-Schöneberg.

1550.

**The King of Bavaria (Ludwig III),
on the Eastern Front on a Vistula River steamboat.**

A forest canteen in a Russian forest. On sale inside would be essentials like soap and extra food, sometimes even alcohol.

DEN
FÜR IHR VATERLAND
GEFALLENEN HELDEN
ZUR EHRE UND ZUM
GEDÄCHTNIS.

JULI 1916
XXI. ARMEEKORPS

July 1916 –
XXI.Armeekorps
memorial to their
fallen.

Medical personnel in the front line pose outside their aid post somewhere in the east during April 1916. In the centre right, the men have created a miniature garden, suggesting this is a quiet area.

January 1916. Kaiser Wilhelm taking the salute as *48 Reserve Division* marches past – part of the German *Südarmee*. The division initially fought on the Western Front but, at the end of November 1914, was transferred to the Eastern Front. It fought in a number of engagements, including the winter 1914 Battle of Łódź, and participated in the pursuit of the Russians after the major battle at Gorlice and Tarnów. The division faced part of the Brusilov Offensive in 1916. From October 1916 to April 1917, it was attached to the Austro-Hungarian *3rd Army*, and was then attached to the Austro-Hungarian *2nd Army*. In May 1917, it returned to the Western Front.

Heinrich Pötzl, an innkeeper in Hackenbuch, was killed in action on 15 June 1916 while serving with *Landsturm Regiment Nr.2*. He was forty at the time of his death and was fighting near Kortovka.

Christmas greetings for 1916 from the Landsturm soldiers at Villa Lina Charlotte in the Carpathians.

Left: **Franz Bachmeier, a miller's son from Aumühle near Pocking, died on 14 February 1916 in a field hospital. He was badly wounded by a shell on 2 February while serving in Russia with *2 Infantry Regiment*, part of *3 Division*.**

Below: **General Otto von Below (centre) was the successful commanding officer of the *Niemen Armee*, later the *8th Army*.**

'Cavalry patrol looking out for the enemy.' Any extra height gave a lookout an advantage: standing on a horse was one way to achieve it. A card sent by a soldier in *11 Landwehr Division*, a sector holding division that fought in Berezina, Olshanka and Krevljanka during 1916.

Austrian light artillery, probably in use for anti-aircraft fire.

A deep and well-constructed dugout in a quiet area where the troops have been for some time – note the birch handrail and cow's head. The men are Landsturm and are there to hold the area, not to fight.

The burial in Russia of an Austrian soldier. The kneeling soldier appears to be taking the dead man's boots off while a civilian grieves. For the others, it is just another death.

Russian prisoners with their escort. As there are only two German guards it is obvious they were not expecting any trouble from their charges. The guards are from *249 Reserve Infantry Regiment*, part of *75 Reserve Division* in *XXXVIII Reserve Corps*. The personnel were predominantly kriegsfreiwillige (wartime volunteers) who did not wait to be called up. From 28 March 1915 to 31 December 1917 it was known as *Beskidenkorps* (Beskids Corps) after the area in Galicia it fought in.

The staff of a casualty station pose outside their dugout. They are clearly identified as medical personnel but would not go to the front line. Possibly the soldier on the right with his apron on is a surgeon.

For those who were lightly wounded, there was no return to Germany even for Christmas. Patients in a hospital in Russia are trying to look as if they are enjoying it.

Unarmed Habsburg soldiers apparently enjoying the vista in full view of the enemy unless these are very well constructed rear area trenches. This photo was sent home by a member of *85 Landwehr Division* who was engaged in positional warfare in the Vishnev sector on the **Berezina, Olshanka and Krevljanka Rivers** from September 1915 to October 1917.

Somewhere in this photograph is Otto Wickel, who at the time had served with his Landwehr unit, *Brigade-Ersatz-Bataillon Nr. 20* since 1914. Taken in Russia on 5 August 1916 when it held the line between the Servech and Shchara rivers.

Winter 1916 in Poland. Three soldiers stand outside an impressive wooden house with a large sign above the entrance: Das Deutsche Haus, probably for rest and recuperation.

German officers' mess in the summer of 1916 in Wolhynien. The region of Volhynia — in German, Wolhynien — is in the northwest corner of Ukraine, west of Kiev. It borders Poland to the west.

Two artillerists on a quiet sector take time-out to read a newspaper.
Their light field gun has apparently two shells left.

A Russian truce
emissary. He has
been blindfolded so
he cannot reveal any
German positions
when he returns to
his own lines.

A 1916 photograph showing those members of *Grenadier-Regiment König Friedrich Wilhelm IV (I. Pommersches) Nr.2*, who had fought in the August 1914 to August 1916 battles. On mobilisation it had fought in France and Belgium before being sent to the east at the end of November 1914 as part of *3 Division*. In 1915 it became part of the newly formed *109 Division* and served in the Baltic region where this picture was taken.

Chapter 4
1917
Mutiny and Revolution

At the beginning of 1917, Russia had reached a point where victory was possible. Winston Churchill described the situation: 'No difficult action was now required; to remain in presence; to lean with heavy weight upon the far-stretched Teutonic line; to hold without exceptional activity the weakened hostile forces on her front; in a word to endure - that was all that stood between Russia and the fruit of general victory.' But it was politics that would decide the outcome of the year: 'the crisis of discontent always begins in the rear' and this was spreading to the front.

On the home front, 'war-weariness manifested itself most obviously in Russia'. The Austro-Hungarian empire, Italy and Russia were 'racing each other to collapse'. By 1917 it was Russia that was certain to win. However, the outcome of the war was still very much in doubt, except perhaps in the Kaiser's mind. He presented unrealistic schemes that senior officers shook their heads at; they took steps to cut him out of the decision-making loop. 'Germany was becoming more and more a military dictatorship every day, with the generals setting not just military policy, but economic and diplomatic policy as well. Their war aims grew more and more ambitious, both cutting off any possibility of a negotiated settlement and committing Germany to fighting harder and longer.'

Time was against Germany. The Habsburg Army was now only capable of static defence and the Ottomans were under pressure from the British and from an Arab revolt. To help their allies, Germany would need to conduct offensives during the year or risk losing the war in 1917.

Offensive activity continued throughout the early months of the year, across the front, even though conditions were severe. Erwin Sello described his transfer to the front near Krewo. 'On the morning of February 21st we marched to Stoj and there entrained in goods-vans. It was lousy cold in the vans, so most of us lay full length, rolled up like mummies in our coats and blankets…It was not much good attempting to sleep in the vans: the hardness of the boards and the cold soon roused one again. On the evening of the 24th we detrained, dead-tired and shaking all over with cold'. His hope of a warm billet was dashed when he was immediately packed into another train – an open-topped field-railway truck. The train moved so slowly that they put their equipment in the trucks and walked by the side of the slow-moving train. When they were too exhausted, they slept on the train because the small wooden walls cut out the wind. Even so the temperature in the truck was -36°C. One man froze to death while on the truck.

Detraining was not any better. 'We looked like ghosts. Our hoods and coat-collars were a mass of ice. The tears which the wind brought to one's eyes were instantly frozen, so that I could hardly see out of mine.' They still had a march to their camp of at least two hours but now had to carry their full kit. 'Ever so many men fell out. Even the fear of being frozen to death couldn't keep the chaps going. They were past caring what happened.' On reaching the camp, Sello, as a NCO, was detailed to go on further. He and his men were to occupy a trench a mile-and-a-half further on. On arrival it was to be prepared for defence. The journey took an hour-and-a-half. Weary and frozen through, they waded through snow-drifts. 'Every few yards one sank up to one's belly in the snow and had to be helped out.' Sello then realised that his left big toe was frozen. He later found out he was the fifteenth man suffering from frostbite.

One possible way forward for a Germany that was suffering from shortages of just about everything might have been a compromise peace settlement in the east. But neither side showed any interest. 'Instead, Russian generals argued for a new offensive in order to take some heat from the western Allies, who were also their primary sources of credit and hardware.' This was in accordance with the Allies' war aims for 1917 – a year of victory over the Central Powers with an offensive in May by all the Entente members. 'Russia would attack along her entire front with some seventy divisions; and vigorous attacks would be launched on Bulgaria by the French, British and Russian forces in the west at Salonika and the Romanians and Russians in the east.' The aim of this was to compel Bulgaria to withdraw from the war.

This willingness of the generals to fight was not matched by the spirit of the people who were suffering from rampant inflation and a shortage of food – food that was available but could not be transported. 'Desertion and indiscipline in the Russian Army was matched by revolutionary sentiment on the home front.'

'The situation at the front deteriorated very rapidly during the spring of 1917. Two factors contributed decisively to the final demoralisation and disorganisation of the Russian armies. One was the historic Order No. 1 issued by the Soviet on March 14th, 1917, which, by inviting the troops to proceed at once to the election of responsible committees, all but destroyed the military discipline.' The second was a very strong desire for peace, again inspired by the Soviets in Petrograd.

'As a result, increasing numbers of troops refused to fight the foreign invader – even endeavouring to fraternise with him – and instead turned their energies and hatred against their own officers. Large numbers of German troops, it must be added, were affected by the same pacifist virus.'

The indiscipline was made worse by army re-organisation. Told to relinquish a third of their men to form new divisions, commanders chose the most troublesome units which became centres of disaffection. Mutinies were threatened and disorders broke out. 'Similar convulsions had shaken the navy, especially the Baltic Fleet where fresh mutinies had broken out in March.'

Thousands evaded the draft; many became anti-war agitators. Strikes and protests increased in number. On 8 March, when a massive wave of strikes began, the writing was on the wall. Troops refused to act against strikers, Cossacks refused to take their rifles with them into working-class districts of Petrograd, and a machine gun unit replaced live with blank ammunition. One regiment shot their officers and joined the strikers. The Duma formed the Provisional Government to deal with the crisis.

The Tsar had been unable to return from the front because the railway system was paralysed by strikes. Workers made sure that he could get no further than Pskov by lifting the lines. At Pskov he was presented with reports of massive indiscipline and widespread unrest. He was told the Duma no longer recognised his authority and the only way to avoid a civil war was to abdicate. By attempting to hand power over to his brother, he did as requested. His brother had little interest in ruling and refused the throne. The Romanov dynasty was over, but this did not mean that Russia was out of the war. Shortly after this event, America entered the war.

While this was happening, the Central Powers missed their chance to end Russian resistance before the Americans joined the war. No offensive materialised because German intelligence did not know what was going on. When it became clear what was happening, they decided on a propaganda rather than military campaign that told the Russian troops to slough off 'their subjection to the warmongering imperialists' and to distrust their officers and the Provisional Government. To help foment the discontent, Lenin was allowed to return to Russia. In Russia the revolution grew apace 'and by April there was every sign of a total breakdown'.

In response to the changes, both Austria and Germany decided on an intensive propaganda campaign at the front. 'Over Easter (a traditional season for fraternization) they encouraged their soldiers to mingle with the enemy. For several weeks hostilities virtually ceased and German and Austrian intelligence officers circulated behind the Russian lines, addressing the soldiers' committees and stressing their wish for peace. When this did not yield the desired results, feelers were put out to the Russian military and political chiefs, again with no success.

General Deniken described what was typical of many sectors during the summer of 1917. 'In a large, open field, as far as the eye can see, run endless lines of trenches, sometimes coming close up to each other, interlacing their barbed-wire fences...The sun has risen long ago, but it is still as death in the field. The first to rise are the Germans. In one place and another their figures look out from the trenches; a few come out on to the parapet to hang out their clothes, damp after the night, in the sun. A sentry in our front trench opens his sleepy eyes, lazily stretches himself, after looking indifferently at the enemy trenches. A soldier in a dirty shirt, bare-footed, with coat slung over his shoulders, cringing under the morning cold, comes out of his trench and plods towards the German positions, where, between the lines, stands a "post-box"; it contains a new number of the German paper, *The Russian Messenger*, and proposals for barter'.

As a result of this rapid change there were two obvious choices for the German Army: a quick offensive, or sit and wait. The latter was the majority choice. The new government in Russia reiterated its commitment to the Allied cause by declaring that it would not sign a separate peace. Very soon afterwards, a new offensive was approved and within two weeks Russian troops were to launch a major attack on the Germans and Austro-Hungarians.

In the limited time available, Brusilov assembled thirty-one divisions and prepared them as best as possible for a major campaign. With no clear guidance about the focus of the campaign, he decided to attack the Austro-Hungarian *Second* and *Third* Armies. 'They guarded the approaches to strategically important oil fields in the Drohobycz area and, beyond them, the symbolic fortress of Lemberg, whose recapture might provide the Provisional Government with the important morale boost it sought.'

Morale on both sides was at a low ebb and the numbers deserting increased every month. The Russians feared a return to the brutality of the Tsar's regime when the death penalty was re-imposed. The Austro-Hungarians, short of men and weapons, were still attempting to recover from their last thrashing at the hands of the Russians.

On 1 July, using the same methods as the 1916 Brusilov offensive, the Russians attacked along a 100 mile front. The main front was thirty miles wide with subsidiary and diversionary attacks making up the remainder.

The Kerenski or Second Brusilov Offensive began very successfully with ethnic origin outweighing imperial loyalty. When Austro-Hungarian Czech troops found they were facing the Russian Czech Legion, they mutinied and refused to fight. Two regiments simply left the Habsburgs, with many joining their comrades on the Russian side. 'The greatest first day success of the offensive came in the capture of a strong point near Brzezany, where Russian forces took more than 10,000 prisoners', many of which were German. The Austro-Hungarian *Second Army* collapsed as did *Eighth Army* with units fleeing in panic, creating a gap forty-five miles long and over twenty miles deep.

Russian forces now had command of the southern approaches to Lemberg, had established bridgeheads across the Lomnica River and driven a wedge between the German and Austro-Hungarian troops. Further south they had cleared most of the Bukovina and advanced to the passes of the Carpathian Mountains.

Not all Russian forces were ready to take part in any hostilities. Some units took no care to repair their trenches or could not do so because so many had deserted. In others old soldiers had been demobilised by the committee and some were on leave. Others had 'been elected members of numerous committees, or gone away as delegates'. One set of delegates had gone to see Kerenski to see if he really had given the orders to advance.

It was a short but successful period. The Russians claimed to have captured over 36,000 prisoners, ninety-three artillery pieces and over 400 machine guns, taken two important river lines and cut Lemberg off bar one road. On 18 July, striking in the direction of Halicz and Dolina, the Russians overwhelmed the Austrian Third Army, advancing up to twenty miles in the centre of a sixty mile front. Large numbers of prisoners were taken, many being disaffected Slav units. The entire *81st Czech Regiment* surrendered and the next day marched through Tarnopol, into captivity, with flags flying, bands playing and a Cossack escort. It would form part of the Czech Legion and fight for the Russians. The advance now threatened the oil wells at Drohobycz, but, as resistance hardened, the advance faltered.

In Petrograd the situation was different: soldiers turned out in their thousands carrying anti-war banners and placards. As the uprising spread, members of the government went into hiding.

Brusilov was removed and replaced by Kornilov. His excessive use of the death penalty for deserters did nothing to improve morale: men continued to desert in droves. While the internal power struggle between Kornilov and Kerenski came to a head, the fighting continued across the eastern front and the Germans were preparing an offensive in the Baltic provinces.

The Russian military triumph was short-lived. The Germans now began to concentrate for their own offensive. On 19 July, a *Südarmee* counter-attack, with nine German and two Austro-Hungarian divisions, 'crashed into the northern flank of the Russian advance. Low on supplies and fully unable to withstand the assault, the Russians began to flee, often in panic'. Tarnopol fell on 26 July and Czernowitz on 1 August. In many places the retreat turned into a rout, and within a few weeks all the gains and more had been lost. Even the use of a Women's Battalion to shame the men could not halt the retreat. Everything gained in the Kerenski offensive and more had been lost, including all of the Bukovina and all but a small strip of Galicia near Brody.

'In the final weeks of July, the Russians lost more than 10,000 men to the Central Powers' losses of just 12,500 men. Central Powers' forces only stopped their pursuit when they ran out of supplies' and when met by a determined Romanian attack.

Regarding the Russian Army as broken, the German Army decided to launch its next attack in the direction of Riga. Artillery Colonel Bruchmüller moved north. His artillery opened fire on 1 September without registering their guns: 20,000 shells, most of them gas shells, without warning. This was followed by storm troops, all volunteers, who crossed the rivers and streams in specially designed boats, directing artillery fire and establishing bridgeheads. *Eighth Army* pushed across the Dvina and within forty-eight hours had nine divisions across the river. Riga was surrounded and fell on the 5th. The Russian Twelfth Army largely disintegrated with the men retreating so quickly only about 9,000 men were taken prisoner. German casualty estimates were as low as 4,200.

In Germany a day of national celebration was ordered and General Hutier, commander of *Eighth Army* was awarded the Pour le Mérite. Hutier then ordered the amphibious assault of the Baltic islands of Ösel, Moon and Dagö. On 12 October, using spotter aircraft to target Russian positions, cruisers and torpedo boats to clear away the Russian surface fleet, and marines to secure landing areas, *42 Infantry Division* was ashore in five hours. The next day Arensburg, the island capital, was occupied and by 20 October all the islands were secured.

'This defeat sealed the fate of the Provisional Government and Kerenski fled to Moscow, leaving Petrograd at the mercy of Lenin and the Bolsheviks, who duly seized power in October.' Peace talks with Bulgaria and Turkey were already under way when, on 20 October, Petrograd received indications that Austria-Hungary also wanted to conclude peace. But this could not save the Provisional Government which was overthrown by a Bolshevik rising.

On 21 November, all Russian Army units received a radio-message that was picked up by German radio-monitors at Brest-Litovsk. 'Soldiers, Peace, the great peace, is in your hands, you will not let the counter-revolutionary generals make peace a failure...peace is in your hands'. After lengthy haggling, the Bolsheviks' armistice became the Peace of Brest-Litovsk. Russia was out of the war.

No longer honour-bound to the western Allies, the new Russian government 'made overtures to the Germans about an armistice'. Trotsky urgently required the fighting to end in order to complete the Bolshevik revolution and stop a civil war. On 5 December, active combat was temporarily ended. Negotiations on a treaty that would end Russia's part in the war then began.

Discussions began at Brest-Litovsk on 17 December. In the meantime German units had crossed the front and redeployed to make any resumption of hostilities easier to begin. They also began negotiations with the Ukrainian government.

'Early negotiations were tense and acrimonious from the start.' The terms of the armistice, the Russians were told, were not for haggling over. They had been beaten and the Germans wanted a victor's peace. As well as land, they also wanted Russian resources to replace those lost by the British blockade. By the end of the year, with the talks still ongoing, the Russians had lost Finland, Poland and the Baltic states.

The events in the east had been closely watched in the west. 'As the months passed in 1917, the grave condition of the Russian Army, and the fear that little more could be expected of it, had caused ever-increasing anxiety to the General Staffs in Paris and London.' The lack of fighting as well as fraternisation were also noted. Even the Kerenski offensive brought them little relief. Its only result was the destruction of the last few reliable elements in the Russian Army. It was obvious to western planners that the collapse of Russia would also mean the end of Romania.

On 11 November, Hindenburg had proposed a Spring offensive in the west. With Russia about to leave the war, this would provide vital numbers of extra troops. Victory in the east would decide the outcome of the war. The decision for 1918 had been taken; only the when and where were undecided.

This possibility had not gone unnoticed in the Allied camp. A memorandum to the British War Cabinet on 9 May clearly spelled out the issue caused by the probability of Russia leaving the war: it 'would increase the German rifle and gun strength on the Western Front to slightly more than that of the Allies'.

On 1 November 1917 the German army on the Western front numbered 3.25 million men. Over the next five months it grew to 4 million, while troop numbers in other theatres fell from 2 to 1.5 million. Most came from the east which provided thirty-eight divisions and, fortunately for them, they mostly went to quieter areas to relieve veteran Western Front men for a strategic reserve. However, many of those transferred simply vanished on route. The trains were slow, usually without toilets, conditions were squalid, meals were irregular and there was little officer supervision. With time on their hands, many decided to demobilise themselves. In autumn 1917, it was estimated that one in ten deserted while moving from east to west. 30,000 fled to neutral countries and up to 50,000 roamed around Berlin. Others just stayed behind the lines, always on the move.

On 3 December, addressing his army commanders, Haig 'informed them that "the general situation on the Russian and Italian fronts, combined with the paucity of reinforcements which we are likely to receive, will in all probability necessitate our adopting a defensive attitude for the next few months. We must be prepared to meet a strong and sustained hostile offensive.' Only days before he spoke, *OHL* had ordered the transfer of troops from the east and other fronts.

In Russia 'the new government permitted army commanders to negotiate local truces, which covered much of the front even before a general armistice with the Central Powers was agreed on 4/15 December…After the ceasefire…the bulk of the remaining troops departed en masse to return to their homes and to take part in the agrarian revolution. Having on the whole hung together through the upheavals since March, the army finally disintegrated'.

A camouflaged heavily-armoured Austro-Hungarian train. In September 1914, Captain Schoeber, chief of the *15th Railway Building Division*, built an armoured train in Galicia. He covered the engine with 8-12 mm thick boilerplates and strengthened the open wagons with rails and thin iron plates. Machine-guns were placed in loopholes to provide both offensive and defensive capability. Captain Kossowicz, chief of the *5th K.u.K. Railway Building Division,* made a second armoured train on the Munkachevo-Stryj line. It consisted of two units that could fight covering each other, with two 80mm cannons that fired headway. This train was so successful that the HQ of the Monarchy (AOK) immediately ordered new trains. On the dissolution of the empire, the trains were taken by Poland, Austria and Czechoslovakia and were still in use in the Second World War.

German occupation staff arrive in Riga to set up their HQ in the Town Hall next to the famous House of the Blackheads. Originally called the New House, it was built in 1334. The house was built as a meeting and celebration venue for different social organisations in Riga. In the 17th century its sole occupants were the cheerful and industrious, mainly German merchants – the Blackheads' Society. It was destroyed during the Second World War and rebuilt in 1999.

Dressing station in the Carpathians during the summer of 1917.

The Kaiser and Prinz Leopold of Bavaria on the Zlota Gora heights in July 1917, after the battle had moved on.

The Kaiser being greeted by the local population during his visit to Tarnopol in July 1917.

A captured equipment collection point near Horodenka, west of Kiev in the Ukraine.

Setting up camp in a field near the damaged bridge over the River Prut at Czernowitz.

POWs being taken to their future home in Austria. That there are no guards to escort them speaks volumes about the state of the Russian army in 1917.

Balloon troops checking the direction and speed of the wind.

A collection point for Russian POWs at Lemberg.

The Russian delegation being greeted on their arrival at Brest-Litovsk on 6 December.

German and Russian peace talks delegations at the negotiating table. 1- Kameneff, 2 – Joffe, 3 – Frau Viecenko, 4 – Rear Admiral Altvater, 5 – Captain Lipsky, 6 – Karachan, 7 – Fokke, 8 – Talat Pasha (Turkish representative), 9 – von Méry, 10 – Prinz Leopold of Bavaria; 11 – Generalmajor Hoffmann, 12 – Oberst Gantschew (Bulgarian Representative), 13 – Commodore Horn, 14 – Captain Hey, 15 – Major Brinkmann, 16 – Major von Kameke, 17 Rittmeister Rosenberg, 18 - Major Mirbach.

Taken in November 1917: 'Music at the meeting point between the positions.' Russian and German fraternisation on the frozen river.

November 1917 – a dance competition on the frozen River Yassyolda.

Moving a division and cyclist brigade plus many other troops required a number of ships. Here men of 42 Division are boarding a ship in Libau.

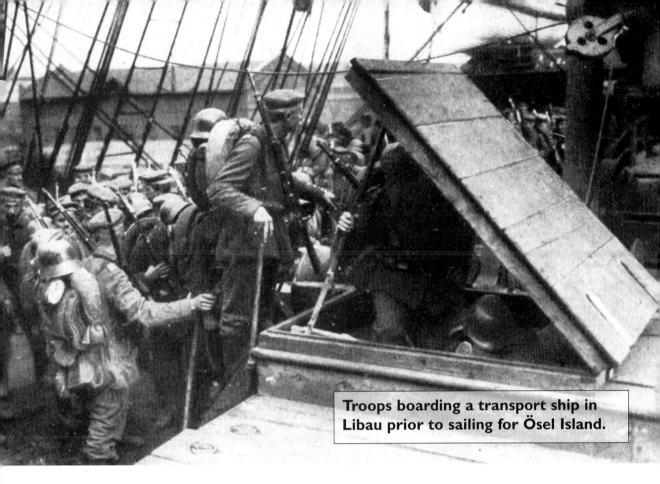

Troops boarding a transport ship in Libau prior to sailing for Ösel Island.

Provisioning a ship in Libau.

Although conditions on board were primitive, the men were well fed before they landed. A goulash cannon on board with expectant troops.

Unloading the artillery for the invasion of Ösel.

Landing artillery baggage and necessities during the invasion of Ösel.

The arrival of 42 _Division_ on the shore of Ösel.

German marines and soldiers setting up quarters on the first day of the invasion of Ösel island in the Gulf of Riga. On 11 October, after extensive naval activity, the first troops landed at Tagalaht, and by 16 October, the island was secured.

Jakobstadt town and market square on the day of capture.

Bringing up the artillery to bombard Jakobstadt. To aid the guns' movement over the marshy ground, a ribbon road of felled trees has been laid down.

The debris left behind by the Russians during their retreat from Riga.

Left: **German troops crossing the destroyed bridge over the Düna.**

Below: **A German Marine-Detachment on board an accommodation boat at the mouth of the Düna near the Russian coastal fortress.**

Captured heavy Russian coastal fortress guns at the mouth of the Düna.

General von Alten, the Governor of Riga.

General von Hutier, the conqueror of Riga. On 3 September 1917, commanding *Eighth Army*, Hutier ended the two-year siege of Riga. He moved his troops to an unexpected sector in the Russian lines, and, using a heavy bombardment prepared by Colonel Bruchmüller and a surprise crossing of the Düna River, took the city. He followed this success with Operation Albion, an amphibious assault (the only successful one of the war) that seized Russian-held islands in the Gulf of Riga.

General Graf von Schmettow, the conqueror of Jakobstadt. He was a cavalry general who had fought on the Western Front before being transferred to the east.

General Hugo von Kathen was in charge of the landings on Ösel. During the war he had a varied career: military governor of Mainz; commanding general of the *XXIII Reserve Corps*; 31 July - 11 November 1918: commander-in-chief of *Eighth Army;* commander of the German troops in Lithuania and Estonia and from February 1919 commander of the German troops in Latvia.

An apparently very warm welcome for the German troops who had defeated the Russians. The officer in the centre is Prince Adolf II. He was the last ruler of the Principality Schaumburg-Lippe in northwest Germany.

The Kaiser with Prinz Leopold of Bavaria inspecting troops in newly-captured Riga.

Triumphal entry by German troops into Riga.

МОСКОВСКАЯ
ХЛѢБО-ПЕ
и КОФЕ
С. К. СЫНЫ

German soldiers outside the cinema in Brest-Litovsk.

With the war temporarily over, more and more troops fraternised. Here German and Russians pose outside a dugout.

German *Infantry Regiment 410*, a part of *Eighth Army*, crossing the River Düna on a newly-made pontoon bridge.

Above: The sender wrote on the back that this showed protection against malaria. The picture was taken in Russia during June 1917.

Left: A hand-coloured photo that clearly shows the difference between the Western and Eastern Fronts. The lack of barbed wire and the depth of the trench would be insufficient protection for troops in France or Belgium.

Artillery in action during the advance through Galicia in July-August 1917.

A medal presentation to machine gunners in *Landwehr Infantry Regiment 23*. Part *of 4 Landwehr Division*, it was at the front in Poland from the early days, and participated in the Gorlice-Tarnów Offensive, crossing the Vistula in July and advancing toward the Bug. It eventually reached the line between the Servech and Shchara rivers near Baranovichi, where it remained in the line until the armistice on the Eastern Front in December 1917.

Infantry Regiment 4 crossing the Düna River at the start of the Battle for Riga.

A summer photograph of the headquarters of *Sanitats Kompagnie 278* in Gutshof Gorgolice (Gorgolice estate).

March 1917 – a mounted escort for two Russian prisoners. Note the guard is wearing the 1914 style headgear.

Men from Nürnberg-Fürth, campaigning in Russia during August 1917. They are a small part of *III. Battalion Bavarian Landwehr Infantry Regiment 10* that was in the newly formed *2 Bavarian Landwehr Division*. It served in the Baltic region near Riga and in September it participated in the Battle of Riga. The division then remained on the line on the Düna River until the armistice on the Eastern Front in December 1917.

Soldiers of the *Solingen Landsturm* in Poland. This is a guard detachment on railway protection detail.

German and Russian sentries meet in No Mans Land during the armistice of 1917. Note the difference in clothing between the two men.

Austro-Hungarian soldiers taking a drink during the Kerenski Offensive in the summer of 1917.

A soldier pays his respects to fallen comrades in the Heroes Cemetery near Wilna.

A card of General von Linsingen sent by a soldier in *Infantry Regiment 82* part of *22 Infantry Division*. It fought initially on the Western Front but was soon sent to the Eastern Front, where it remained until October 1917.

A bicycle company moving to
the front through the ruins of a town. Although the
card is dated 1917 the soldiers are still wearing pickelhauben.

Christmas in the field,
1917. A medic in the entrance to his dugout.

A behind-the-lines billet – an attempt to give the men some time away from the front when there was no leave. This is the Soldatenheim (leave home) for *III.Battalion, Landwehr Regiment 103,* part of *46 Landwehr Division,* a newly formed division.

Russian inhabitants of Ösel Island.

A machine gun section in June 1917 somewhere in the east.

Zensiert
Paul Hoffmann & Co.
Berlin-Schöneberg.

Waffenruhe an der Ostfront.
Beim Tauschhandel.

1602.

Exchanging newspapers and bartering on the Eastern Front in late 1917. The numerals on the German soldier's collar indicate he is a Landsturm soldier from the East Prussian Army Command.

Josef Hager, an Austrian mountain soldier, died of wounds on 8 August 1917 at the age of twenty-six.

Crossing the Düna near Riga at the start of the September battle.

Russian prisoners being given treatment at a dressing station after the battle on the Zlota-Gora heights.

The arrival of the Russian peace delegation at Brest-Litovsk on 18 November 1917.

Chapter 5
1918
Peace in War

As the New Year started, the Brest-Litovsk twenty-eight day armistice between Russia and Central Powers that began at noon on 17 December was still in operation. However, the peace negotiations were not. They had stalled when the Bolsheviks were told that Poland and the Baltic states would become independent.

The renewable armistice meant that both sides would stay in their respective positions. No strategic troop movements were to be allowed unless they were already in progress. This was intended to keep German divisions in the east, but no movement could be policed, and anyway it was too late. *OHL* had issued transfer orders before it was signed. In order to spread unrest, the Bolsheviks wanted fraternisation between the armies, but this had only been allowed on a restricted basis.

While the talks were under way, the Germans signed a separate treaty with the Ukraine. In return for grain and minerals, they promised not to annex the new state. Both the Austrians and Germans also released their Ukrainian prisoners of war. The outcome of all this was unexpected and unwelcome. Furious at the loss of the Ukraine, the Russians invaded: the result was civil war, the assassination of Field Marshal von Eichhorn (military governor of the Ukraine) and the tying down of 650,000 men to maintain order, men that could have been used on the Western Front.

Although the Russians needed the treaty, Trotsky was not prepared to accept the Ukrainian treaty and walked out of the negotiations on 10 February. The Kaiser's response to the impasse was to divide European Russia among German Royal families: Poland went to the House of Württemberg, Lithuania to the House of Saxony, Finland to his son Oskar and the remainder to his own House of Hohenzollern. The Habsburgs got nothing.

On 13 February, at the Bad Homburg Crown Council, it was decided that there was a need to safeguard Ukrainian food supplies and compel the Bolsheviks to sign the peace. To achieve this, the German columns would need to move forward again. This was codenamed Operation Faustschlag.

On 18 February, the Central Powers started a major three-pronged offensive with 53 divisions. 'The northern force advanced from Pskov towards Narva, the central force pushed towards Smolensk, and the southern force towards Kiev.' Opposition was light: the Russians had been preparing for peace.

In the south, Ottoman troops renewed their attacks in the Caucasus Mountains. Here there had been constant fighting since November 1914 and, with the collapse of Imperial Russia, the Ottomans moved rapidly in to fill the void. A special force was created for this: the Army of Islam. The purpose of this military unit was to mobilise Islamic supporters, in the Transcaspian and Caucasian regions, to advance toward Shatt al-Arab through Persia, and to entrap British forces in Mesopotamia for establishing a Pan-Turanic Empire. At the end of the war, although the Ottomans had lost most of their empire, they did retain the territory regained in eastern Anatolia and had beaten the British Dunsterforce at Baku in September.

'The northern force, consisting of 16 divisions, captured the key Daugavpils junction on the first day. This was soon followed by the capture of Pskov and securing Narva on 28 February. The central forces of the *10th Army* and *XLI corps* advanced towards Smolensk. On 21 February Minsk was captured together with the headquarters of the Western Army Group. The Southern forces broke through the remains of the Russian Southwestern Army Group, capturing Zhitomir on 24 February. Kiev was secured on 2 March, one day after the Ukrainian Central Rada troops had arrived there.'

Moving quickly, German troops captured hundreds of kilometres, key cities fell and the Germans made ready to move into Bessarabia and the Crimea. Helsinki fell, its garrison surrendering en masse, resulting in the Russians agreeing to evacuate Finland. The advance continued into the Ukraine and along the Baltic, demonstrating to Lenin and Trotsky that they had no choice but to sign the German terms.

'Central Powers armies had advanced over 150 miles within a week, facing no serious resistance. German troops were now within 100 miles of Petrograd, forcing the Soviets to transfer their capital to Moscow. The rapid advance was described as a "Railway War" (*der Eisenbahnfeldzug*). General Hoffmann wrote in his diary: 'It is the most comical war I have ever known. We put a handful of infantrymen with machine guns and one gun onto a train and rush them off to the next station; they take it, make prisoners of the Bolsheviks, pick up few more troops, and so on. This proceeding has, at any rate, the charm of novelty.'

On 3 March, the Treaty of Brest-Litovsk was signed, ceding two-and-a-half million square kilometres of territory that included the Baltic states, Belorussia, Finland and Poland to the Germans. The Turks gained parts of Armenia. In a legal sense, the military power of Russia was out of the war, and, with ratification of the peace treaty on 15 March, in Allied eyes, Russia became, not quite an ally of Germany but certainly its helper. This meant that Allied intervention in Russia was now permissible.

Hundreds of thousands of POWs were also to be released, but of these only 151,700 were German. Most were in poor physical condition and they arrived only slowly in Germany. Before they could be sent west, they needed to be quarantined for up to three months in case they spread Bolshevism, and also to re-build their strength and train them.

Germany took control over ninety per cent of Russia's coal, half of the heavy industry and sixty-two million people. For the planned offensive in the west they took rifles, artillery and ammunition. There was also food and oil. By October, 'the Germans had taken away 47,174 tonnes of grain, 30,844 tonnes of beet sugar, 45 million eggs, 53,000 horses and 48,000 hogs.' However, to maintain order and take the materials meant that they had to leave nearly a million men on the Eastern Front.

These men were needed in the west, and would gradually be moved, almost to the very end of the war.

This 'continuing presence on the Eastern Front dwarfed its other commitments, and after March 1918 transfers from Russia to the west slowed down, two more divisions being moved in May but no more until the autumn'. However, there were still thirty-four divisions in the east in early November. Their presence in the east 'constituted an under-utilised reserve when manpower was desperately needed' - even if the best had already been taken.

For the March offensive 'the highest quality eastern units were transported, including guards divisions, and those left behind lost their men aged under thirty-five and fell well below strength, as well as sacrificing many of their horses.' The eastern army, on the eve of the March offensive had 40,095 officers, 1,004,955 men, and 281,770 horses; in contrast the western army had respectively 136,618, 3,38,288, and 710,827. Although mainly mediocre, the eastern army was numerically strong, but by July had fallen to around 500,000.

German forces were ordered to halt except in the Ukraine where they took Odessa and Nikolayev. To occupy the newly-captured territory, *Armee Gruppe Eichhorn* was formed at Kiev with eighteen divisions.

Although the Peace Treaty had been ratified, German troops did not stop fighting in the Ukraine. In May, part of the Black Sea fleet was seized and Rostov was occupied. Heavy fighting in June resulted in the Austrians taking 10,000 POWs. However, as the needs of the Western Front grew, more and more divisions left Russia and the fighting was considerably reduced. By the end of the war, much of the policing of captured territory was being carried out by cavalry with minimal support. To further reduce the need for manpower in the east, Germany signed a supplementary peace treaty with Russia.

'For Ludendorff it made little sense to draw further troops from Russia to strengthen his hand in France, for much of the purpose of the western campaign was to maintain Germany's Brest-Litovsk gains.' Without the protecting garrison, the gains would crumble. It had also cost hundreds of thousands of men taking the territory: it had to be held.

In fact, German ambitions expanded and there was little that the Allies could do to stop them. The ambitions 'centred on two drives towards Scandinavia and the Black Sea. In the north German soldiers landed in Finland in April, to assist the anti-Bolshevik forces in the Finnish Civil War. They took Helsingfors (Helsinki) and defeated the Reds within weeks.'

On the surface this was a military action, but underneath there were political and economic undertones. The Germans wanted a friendly government in place, naval bases on the Baltic and Barents Seas and access to raw material like nickel. It also gave them a base for further operations.

In April, German troops occupied the Crimea to control the ports, seize supplies and protect the German settlers there: during the summer they discussed plans to make the peninsula a German colony. At the same time the Ottoman Empire was expanding through the Caucasus, breaking up the newly independent state of Transcaucasia into Armenia, Azerbaijan and Georgia. In May Germany occupied Georgia which it needed for its minerals. The *OHL* idea was to form a joint force with the Turks, control the Caspian Sea, co-operate with Afghanistan, attack British interests in Persia and threaten India. However, relatively few German troops went to the Caucasus or Crimea; most were swallowed up by the Ukraine.

This committal to the Caucasus by the Ottoman Empire was to have severe repercussions on its ability to conduct war in the Middle East. With half their available forces, including most of their best soldiers who had served in Galicia and Romania, in the region, there were insufficient troops to fight the British and garrison important Turkish cities.

The Ukraine was central to Germany's survival. It would provide food and, like Georgia, contained large quantities of raw materials. And both, as Christian states, needed protecting from Ottoman expansion. This emergent eastern empire would 'sustain Germany in the next war'. The occupation kept the occupying troops fed and opened the possibility of access to the Baku oilfields, the most productive in the world.

In the summer Operation Keystone was drawn up. This was a plan to move German troops from Finland and occupy Kronstadt and Petrograd, replace the Bolsheviks with a reactionary regime and attack the Allied forces landing at Murmansk. Only imminent defeat in the west curtailed the operation.

In November 1918 Russian security was restored and its annexed provinces returned, in some cases only temporarily before their full independence. On 11 November there were twenty-six German divisions spread across a front from Finland to Georgia, with seven Habsburg divisions in the Ukraine. Five days later the evacuation of the Ukraine began and on 18 November they left Estonia.

While the Central Powers were no longer involved in the fighting on the Eastern Front, it would be some considerable time before there was peace in the region. Indeed, as they withdrew, they left Russia in a state of civil war and Poland moving troops to its borders against any potential Bolshevik threat.

The hearses carrying two German soldiers killed in the fighting against the Bolsheviks near Tiflis in Georgia.

German soldiers, released from Russian captivity, in the funeral procession for two dead German soldiers.

German and White Russian officers in the funeral procession for the two German soldiers killed near Tiflis.

3

Deputation of Georgian soldiers in the funeral procession for two dead German soldiers.

4

German luggage convoy advancing near Tiflis in Georgia.

German troops in Tiflis. Georgia, with German backing, declared itself as an independent state when the Russian Empire collapsed. The proximity of German troops to the oilfields at Baku caused considerable friction between the Turks and Germans. Fighting broke out that only stopped when Germany threatened to stop backing the Ottoman Empire.

The formal signing of the peace agreement with the new republic of the Ukraine

German troops on the move in the Baltic. Crossing the railway line from Riga to Petrograd on the main road through the hilly countryside of Livonia – the Baltic lands above Lithuania.

Luggage sleighs on the advance to Dorpat in Estonia.

A captured Russian equipment dump prior to recycling to Austro-Hungarian and rear-echelon troops.

Mail for the garrison on Ösel Island.

An Austro-Hungarian war dog examination centre. These dogs are being checked out for health prior to their potential use in the military.

Exchange of prisoners at Sassnitz in northern Germany.

An Austrian woman who had been fighting on the Russian front with the *Polish Legion* was part of the 1918 prisoner exchange.

**GeneralFeldmarschall von Eichhorn (centre), General von Bredow
(centre right) with their staff walking through Minsk in the Ukraine.**

**German troops resting near lake Preipus in Estonia
before moving north.**

Field censorship had been very lax until late in 1917 and even then, by British standards, it was still lax. It was mostly used to find out how the soldiers felt about the war rather than remove information about where the soldier was stationed.

A low-key German presence at a rally in Helsinki after the Russian-backed Reds had been defeated. The war was fought from 27 January to 15 May 1918 between the forces of the Social Democrats - the Reds, and the forces of the non-socialist, conservative-led Senate, - the Whites, who were assisted by 13,000 German soldiers, from the beginning of April 1918. The men in civilian dress with French helmets and armbands are Finnish White Guard soldiers.

Finnish White Guard with German
railway defence soldier patrol the line
from Helsinki to Hangö

Advancing German railway pioneers on the line from Helsinki to Hangö.

In the occupied areas, law was dispensed by the military. Here a woman is being questioned in front of a military tribunal with the authority to give capital sentences for minor wrongdoings as a warning to others.

Untouched by the war, the Ukraine after the armistice. The Central Powers moved there even though it was land they had not taken during the war. Here Austro-Hungarian troops arrive in Kamienic-Podolski in southwest Ukraine.

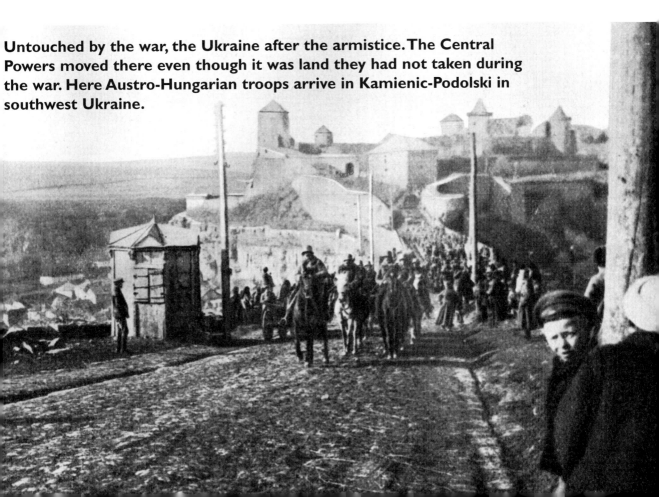

Austrians returning from the front – every available space is taken because of the constant shortage of transport.

Before the spring thaw in 1918. German shock troops are being attacked by Russian troops.

German engineers building a replacement bridge over the Dniester. Note the destroyed bridge in the background.

Captured Russian armoured cars in the centre of Zloczow in the Ukraine.

The Kaiser and his entourage on the Dune Quai at Riga.

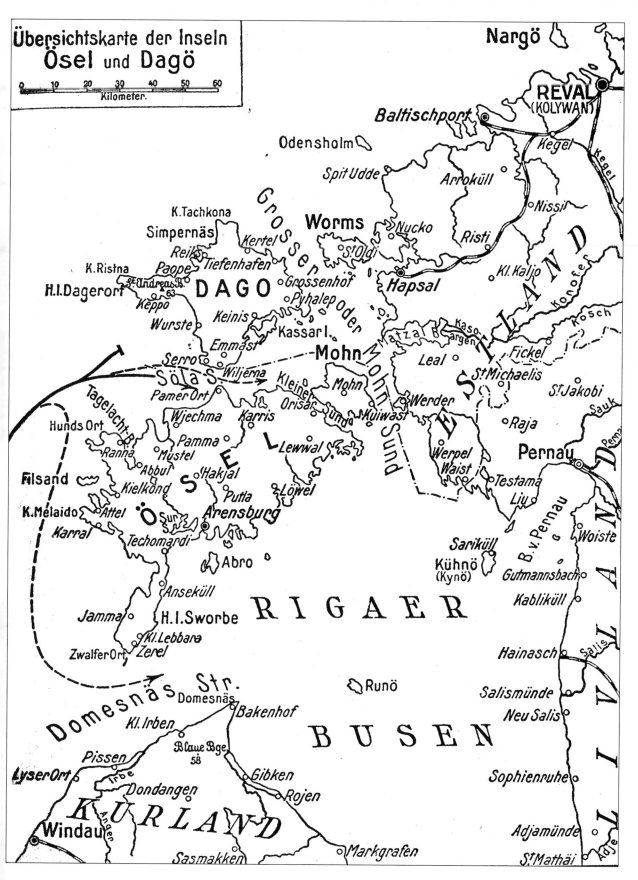

Map of the Baltic islands captured by the Germans during Operation Albion.

Naval and army sentries guarding the Dünemunde harbour entrance.

Viewing the first prisoners taken during the Ösel Island landings.

The Kaiser with von Eichhorn leaving the Orthodox Church in Wilna, the Lithuanian capital.

Prince Leopold, Commander of all forces in the east, looking over a battlefield with his Chief of Staff, Colonel Hoffmann, and his staff.

Feldmarschall von Böhm-Ermolli
and his divisional commanders
during their advance into the
Ukraine.

Infanterist Alois Ellinger
was serving with *K.u.K.
Infantry Regiment Nr.1*
when he died of wounds in
a field hospital in Russia.
Before his death on 9
September 1918 he had
been awarded the Bronze
bravery medal and the
Troop Cross.

The spring thaw in Russia. A Landwehr soldier stands in the newly thawed ground in a deserted village.

A Landsturm NCO, winner of the Iron Cross Second Class, is wearing his marksman lanyard. He is a soldier in Landsturm Regiment 12, Army Corps Command 14, from Baden.

Some of the Landwehr men left in Russia after the best were selected for service in the offensives in the west.

Austro-Hungarian soldier wearing the bronze medal for bravery. His collar badges indicate he is a member of the anti-aircraft artillery.

Asiatic Russian soldiers working for the Germans as labourers in October 1918.

A partly camouflaged field howitzer in action in the Ukraine, even though the war is over.

Much use was made of cavalry during the advance in the Ukraine. Most of the soldiers in such units were older men and the units they fought with were unsuitable for use on the Western Front.

No longer enemies. German and Russian soldiers fraternise during the winter of 1917/1918.

German troops in position in Estonia 1918.

Landwehr troops ready for action in Russia during February 1918.

Landsturm soldiers holding the line. Note the neat firewood pile at the front left – obviously an area where there was little movement.

Brest-Litowsker Strasse in Kowel

Brest-Litovsk Street in Kowel in early 1918. Little is happening, so the few soldiers around are happy to pose for the camera.

A telephone station in a Ukrainian forest.

A mass latrine in use by Landwehr men somewhere in the east. The sort of photo that would not have been possible in the British Army.

A meeting of high-ranking officers in a forest clearing during summer 1918 in Lithuania. All the officers are wearing the old-style helmet so there is obviously no chance of enemy fire hitting the forest.

Leutnant Hans Röhrner, a bank official in Vilshofen, Bavaria, died in a field hospital on 17 December 1918 at the age of twenty-eight-and-a-half. During his service he had been awarded the Iron Cross Second Class and the Military Achievement Cross.

A 21cm mortar in its firing pit being readied for firing.

Chronology of the Russian Front 1914 – 1918

1914

29 July Partial Russian mobilisation against Austria. Tsar fails to stop full mobilisation.

30 July Tsar signs general mobilisation order to start 4 August.

31 July German decision to mobilise.

1 August German general mobilisation declared at 1700 hours followed by declaration of war against Russia at 1910 hours.

2 August Poland invaded by Germans, who, by the next day, occupy Kalish, Chenstokhov and Bendzin. East Prussia entered by Russian raiders near Schwidden. Libau, in Baltic Province of Latvia, bombarded by German light cruisers *Augsburg* and *Magdeburg*.

5 August Austria declares war on Russia. Russo-German cavalry skirmish at Soldau in East Prussia.

6 August Polish Legion invades Russian Poland.

7 August Russian car patrols in East Prussia.

10 August Austrians invade Poland from Galicia aiming for Lublin and Kielce. Tilsit in East Prussia is reached by Russian cavalry.

12 August Russian 1 Cavalry Division crosses into East Prussia and takes Marggrabowa.

14 August Russian Third Army defeats Austrians at Sokal inside Austrian frontier.

15 August Ten Austrian cavalry divisions cross the Russian Frontier on a 250 mile front but achieve little.

17 August Russians invade East Prussia on a thirty-five mile front. Against orders *I.Korps* commander forces battle at Stallupönen, five miles inside the border. Before his forces retire on Gumbinnen, 3,000 Russians are captured.

18 August Only token resistance offered by Austrians against Russian attack in Galicia.

19 August Russian Second Army invades East Prussia from the south. Austrian advance in Poland is held but Russians evacuate threatened town of Kielce.

20 August Battle of Gumbinnen. Although Russian forces sustained greater casualties, the German attack is held twenty-five miles from border.

22 August Russian forces capture Soldau and Neidenburg in East Prussia.

23 August Russians advance now west of Königsberg taking Angerburg at northern end of Masurian Lakes. At the first Battle of Krasnik, southwest of Lublin in Poland, the Austrian *Third Army* pushes the Russian Fourth Army back three miles. In Galicia, Cossacks take Chertkov rail station and capture Austrian guns at River Sereth crossing.

24 August Russian attack forces defenders back ten miles, capturing Frankenau.

25 August Russian orders broadcast without cipher. Double envelopment of Russian attack ordered. Austrian troops take 6,000 POWs in their advance on Lublin. Russians retreat four miles.

26 August Battle of Tannenberg in East Prussia – Russians evacuate newly captured Allenstein, creating a gap in their line. In Poland the Austrian *Fourth Army* fought the Russian Fifth Army in the Battle of Zamosc-Komarow and in the first Battle of Lemberg two Austrian divisions retreat twenty-five miles back to Lemberg.

27 August Austrian *Fourth Army* in Poland takes Zamosc but Cossacks rout Austrian cavalry divisions. In Galicia the Russians capture Tarnopol and Halicz. Russian 1 Cavalry Division captures Korschen rail junction but Russian left wing is turned and Soldau taken.

28 August Russians under Samsonov in East Prussia retreat but Rennenkampf's troops take Rastenburg. In Poland *15 Austrian Division* destroyed by Russian V Corps losing 4,000 POWs and twenty guns but Russian 61 Division is routed by Austrian *XIV.Korps*.

29 August Russian troops caught in pincer movement at Willenburg near the Russian border.

30 August In East Prussia the Russians retake Neidenburg. Austrian forces take Krasnostav, forty miles inside Poland. To stop threat of encirclement, Russian Fifth Army retreats. In Galicia, fourteen Austrian divisions are routed on the River Gnila Lipa by twenty-two Russian divisions. The Russian troops advance eighteen miles.

31 August Neidenburg captured from Russians. In Poland, Russian Fifth Army successfully avoids encirclement but loses forty per cent of men and over 150 guns. The 40,000 Austrian casualties include eight generals. Russian attacks break the Austrian line near Halicz in Galicia. Austrian losses for first month of war are fifteen per cent of total 1914 losses.

1 September Russians retreat to the River Bug but push Austrians back near Lemberg.

2 September Battle of Lemberg ends with Austrians evacuating the city with the loss of 130,000 men. Austrian *Fourth Army* attack, with thirteen divisions on Lublin, held by fourteen Russian divisions.

3 September Lemberg occupied.

4 September Russians lose Mlawa in Poland to attack from East Prussia.

5 September Austrian *II.Korps* at Tomashov defeated by Russian Fifth Army.

6 September Russian defence on River Vyeprj breaks Austrian attack. In the Battle of Grodek, attacking Austrian troops panic.

7 September Russian XXII Corps routed in the Biala area of East Prussia. Austrian forces beaten during Battle of Tarnaka and are ordered to retreat two days later to San. Russian cavalry reaches the Carpathians and reformed Russian Fifth Army resumes its advance. Opening moves in the First Battle of the Masurian Lakes.

8 September Silesian Landwehr Corps forced over the River Vistula with loss of 8,000 men. In the Second battle of Lemberg Austrian troops are beaten by Russians. Mikolajow in the Carpathians captured by Brusilov's army.

9 September Russians cut off near Lötzen in East Prussia losing 5,000 as POWs.

10 September Russians cover their retreat in East Prussia, ninety-five miles in fifty hours, with a counter-attack. They also evacuate Insterburg. Austrians fare badly at the Second Battle of Krasnik and in Galicia their left flank is turned.

11 September General Austrian retreat ordered as Russians close in on Grodek.

12 September Russians evacuate Tilsit and Germans reach Wirballen and Suvalki in Russia. Grodek taken as Austrians continue their retreat.

13 September Pursuit delayed by Russian rearguards at Vilkoviski.

14 September Russians hold oilfields at Drohobycz and cross River San in pursuit of retreating Austrians.

15 September First Battle of the Masurian Lakes ends with the Russians back in Russia preparing to resist on the Niemen river. In the Bukovina region the Russians occupy the capital – Czernowitz.

16 September *Ninth Army* formed to cover Silesia between the River Oder and the Polish frontier against Russian attacks. Russians advance on Przemysl in Galicia.

18 September Przemysl shelled for the first time.

20 September Raid by Russian Cavalry Corps north of the Vistula is diverted by a German advance. On the East Prussian frontier the Russians abandon Augustovo and their fortress at Osovyets is besieged.

21 September Russians driven across River Niemen but take Jaroslav in Galicia.

22 September *Ninth Army* starts arriving north of Cracow in Poland. Russians continue their advance on Przemysl.

24 September First siege of Przemysl begins.

26 September The two-day Battle of the Niemen begins with the Russians stopping attempted crossings and blocking assaults on Osovyets. Russians occupy Rzeszov on the River Wistock. Austrians reform their front east of the River Dunajec.

28 September *Ninth Army* attacks from near Cracow to aid Austrians. Russians seize the Dukla and Uzsok passes in the Carpathians, capture Krosno and make a cavalry raid into Hungary.

30 September Ninth Army advances at around ten miles a day, entrenching at Kielce.

1 October Start of the Battle of Augustovo. Russians recover the town and attack the retreating Germans.

2 October Russians recover Miriampol on the East Prussian frontier.

3 October In north Hungary the Russians capture Maramaros-Sziget.

4 October Austro-German offensive towards Warsaw begins and Austrians take Opatow.

6 October General Russian retreat in Galicia and Poland.

7 October Russian cavalry raiders leave north Hungary and Austrians retake Maramaros-Sziget.

8 October Russians retake Lyck. General der Infanterie François replaces General Schubert in charge of *Eighth Army*.

9 October Austrians relieve Przemysl. In Poland joint attack force approaches the Ivangorod fortress on the River Vistula.

10 October Russian cavalry again raid north Hungary. Russians defeated south of Warsaw at Grojec. German troops capture Lodz.

11 October Austrians recover Jaroslav and Germans take Sochaczew on River Bzura. Three Russian armies begin attempts to cross the River Vistula.

12 October Troops advancing on Warsaw ordered to dig-in.

13 October Russians forced out of Lyck. Russian Third and Eighth Armies south of Przemysl. The Battle of Chyrow begins in heavy rain. Many of the Austrian troops are suffering from cholera.

14 October Germans take Mlawa.

15 October Russians prepare to evacuate Warsaw as First Battle of Warsaw begins. Four Russian armies attacked by four corps.

17 October Arrival of Russian reinforcements stops the attacking force from taking the city.

18 October Austrians attempt without success to cross the River San. In Poland, Ludendorff decides to order a retreat.

19 October Germans cross the River Vistula at Josefor.

20 October German troops begin planned retreat form Warsaw and abandon the siege of Ivangorod.

21 October At the Battle of Kasimiryev, Russians destroy German bridgehead on the River Vistula.

22 October In a day of heavy fighting Austrian forces take and then lose Czernowitz. During the night a Russian corps crosses the River Vistula.

23 October Russians advance in Poland and in Galicia retake Jaroslav.

24 October Arrival of reinforcements saves Cavalry Corps from Russian attack.

26 October Russian Fourth and Ninth Army attack along Petrokov-Radom line forces the Austrian *First Army*, which loses 40,000 men, to retreat. German troops continue their planned retreat destroying rail installations as they withdraw.

28 October Austrians re-supply the fortress at Przemysl but lose Sambor. Russians recover Lodz and Radom.

29 October Turkey enters the war on Central Powers side. Turkish fleet bombards Russian bases in Sevastopol, Feodosya, Yalta, Odessa and Novorossiysk.

30 October Russians take Stanislau and defeat Germans at Bakalaryevo.

31 October Snow-storms impede fighting. First day of the Battle of Opatowka. Russian offensive begins on the Caucasus front.

1 November German retreat in Poland ending and Hindenburg made C-in-C of German Eastern Front troops. Turkey declares war on the Allies.

2 November Russian Tenth Army re-invades East Prussia. Battle of Chyrow ends with Russian victory and Austrian retreat during the night. Russia and Serbia declare war on Turkey. Russian I Caucasus Corps crosses Turkish border at five points.

3 November Austro-Germans defeated by Russian Fourth Army at Kielce. *Ninth Army* transferred north for attack on Warsaw. Russian I Caucasus Corps occupies Bayazid.

4 November In twelve days of fighting at Jaroslav the Austrian Army is beaten, losing 19,000 POWs and forty guns. Russians occupy Diyadin and are up to seventeen miles over Turkish border. First Battle of Köprüköy against the Russians.

5 November Austrian *First Army* retreats towards Cracow to save itself. German HQ retreats from Szestochowa.

6 November Start of the Battle of Goritten in East Prussia.

7 November General François replaced as C-in-C of *Eighth Army* by General Below. Russians bombard Turkish ports in the Black Sea.

8 November Austrian HQ moved to Teschen, west of Cracow. Russian success in East Prussia: re-enter Eydtkuhnen and Stallupönen and advance into the Imperial Romintern Forest. Austrian *Fourth Army* advances to River Dunajec and sends help to *First Army*.

9 November Recently formed *Army Detachment Woyrsch* evacuates Kalish and Chenstokhov. A Russian cavalry raid on Silesia penetrates twenty miles and cuts railway line at Pleschen. Battle of Köprüköy in Armenia. Russian advance on Erzerum blocked.

10 November Russian Eleventh Army resumes siege of Przemysl and in East Prussia re-enters Goldap. In response to continued Russian attacks, the Austrians switch five divisions from the Carpathians to help cover Silesia and four corps from the Western Front are promised to boost the Eastern Front.

11 November Second offensive against Russian-held Warsaw starts. In three days of fighting the Russian V Siberian Corps loses fifteen guns and 12,000 POWs. In Armenia four Turkish divisions counter-attack Russian flanks and force a retreat.

12 November Further Russian successes: they enter Johannisburg south of the Masurian Lakes and occupy Miechow near Cracow.

13 November Russians occupy Dunayetz and threaten Cracow but are beaten off by the fortress at Thorn.

14 November First day of the Battle of Kutno which drives a wedge between the Russian First and Second Armies.

15 November As a result of the fighting at Kutno, the Russian Second and Fifth Armies retreat to a line between Gumbin and Lodz. Second Russian invasion of north Hungary begins. In Armenia Turkish irregulars wipe out a Russian battalion near Batumi.

16 November The Austrian offensive from Cracow makes only limited gains. Russian rearguards at Vlotslavek and Kutno fail to halt attackers. Russian II Turkestan Corps saves I Caucasus Corps and stabilises front in Armenia.

17 November Fighting continues around Plotsk in Poland.

18 November Russian troops near Lodz encircled on three sides: retreat order countermanded. Further fighting north of Cracow. In East Prussia Russian forces at Soldau are beaten.

19 November After successful attacks against Russian positions in Mykanow and Klekoty, the Austrians are blocked by the Russian Fourth Army. Arrival of Austrian *Fifth Army* after forced marches save their *Second Army*.

20 November Russian document cipher captured but replacement solved by Austrians within a few days. Fighting continues at Lodz with Russian infantry superiority at nearly two-to-one.

22 November After breaching Russian line Lowicz-Skiernievitse, German troops move on Lodz but are short of ammunition. The 60,000 troops surrounded at Brzeziny, by the 6th Siberian Division, retreat during the evening. Austrians defeated on the Cracow-Chenstokhov front losing 6,000 POWs. Ottoman troops withdraw from Köprüköy which is re-occupied by the Russians.

23 November Isolated troops launch a breakout attempt through Russian line Rzgov-Koliuszki southeast of Lodz.

24 November 6th Siberian Division destroyed during unsuccessful defence of Brzeziny.

25 November Artillery duels begin at Przemysl and Austrians cease offensive in Galicia after taking 26,000 POWs with a loss of 55,000 casualties. Russians continue raids into Hungary. Russian encirclement near Lodz fails when troops break out through a four-mile gap capturing 16,000 Russians and sixty-four guns.

27 November Hindenburg promoted to Feldmarschall.

28 November Russians secure Carpathian passes. Austrian *XI.Korps* retreats in Galicia and Austrian *Third Army* forced back in north Hungary.

30 November Smaller Russian force checks attack during the Battle of Lowicz-Sanniki until ordered to retreat to shorter line behind River Bzura on 6 December.

1 December Fierce fighting in Lodz suburbs. In north Hungary Russians take and then lose Bartfeld in the Carpathians. During the Battle of Limanowa-Lapanov, the Austrian *Fourth Army* stops Russian advance on Cracow. Russians take Bashkai and Sarai in Armenia.

2 December Russians occupy Bartfeld but continue to be checked near Cracow.

4 December Russian front broken at Llov.

6 December Russians begin retreat to the Bzura-Ravka river line after evacuating Lodz.

7 December Russians attack in East Prussia and bombard Cracow forts. In Poland Second Battle of Warsaw begins with new German offensive. Russians repulse Turkish attacks south of Batumi.

8 December Although Russians reinforce their Third Army, the Austrians, commanded by Feldmarschall-Leutnant Roth, managed to regain some ground.

9 December First ground attacks at Przemysl and heavy fighting around Mlava and Petrokov.

10 December Although heavily attacked and losing 4,000 as POWs, the Austrian line near Lapanow holds.

11 December Russians evacuate Lovich after repelling attack.

12 December Austrians retake Nowa Sacz and Dukla Pass in the Carpathians.

15 December On the River Bzura front, heavy fighting near Sokhachev. Attempt to break out by Austrians at Przemysl fails.

16 December Russian stand on Bzura-Ravka-River Pilica line ends their retreat in Poland.

17 December The Battles of Lowicz-Sanniki and Limanowa-Laponov end with the latter stopping the Russians taking Cracow. Austrians take Petrokov.

20 December Russians defeat Turks near Lake Van.

21 December Russians stop all but two attempts to cross their line on the Bzura river which are pushed back the next day. Turkish winter offensive begins as ten divisions attack in Armenia. 64,000 Russians driven back and Köprüköy is recovered.

22 December Turkish Third Army launches an offensive in the Caucasus.

23 December Russians retreat twelve miles and abandon Olta. Turks take 750 POWs and six guns.

24 December Turkish troops inside Russian frontier at Bardiz.

25 December Fighting continues with Christmas truce in some areas. Russians retake Carpathian passes at Dukla and Lupkow. Austrians stopped at Tarnow in Galicia at the end of the Austro-German offensive. Russians retreat in Armenia. Turkish *3 Division* captures Ardahan.

26 December In Armenia the Battle of Sarikamish begins. Heavy Turkish losses. Turkish *X Corps* in twenty-five hour horror march.

27 December Russians beat back German attacks on River Ravka.

28 December German retreat from River Bzura. Turkish *30 Division* occupies Alisofu isolating Russians.

29 December Austrian retreat in Galicia. Further Turkish attacks repulsed and they lose Alisofu. Night attack troops annihilated. Between 29 December and 2 January, thousands of Turkish soldiers die because of inadequate winter clothing and field shelters while crossing the Allahüekber Mountains and during the attack and retreat against the Russians.

30 December As Russians follow-up retreat, Germans fight rearguard actions at Bolimow and Inovlodz.

31 December Further Russian raids in Hungary through Carpathian passes. Turkish *XI Corps* attacks on Russian border.

1915

1 January Russians advance in Bukovina and at Uzsok Pass. Turkish *X Corps* begins retreat

2 January Fighting near Gorlice and Russian successes on the Bzura and Ravka rivers. Russians launch a counter-offensive against the Turkish *Third Army* in the Caucasus.

3 January Russians occupy Suczava in the Bukovina. Siberian Cossacks retake Ardahan and 1,300 POWs.

4 January The Battle of Sarikamish ends with the destruction of Turkish *IX Corps*.

6 January Russians occupy Kimpolung (Bukovina) and reach Hungarian frontier.

7 January In Poland heavy German attacks on lower Ravka are repulsed. Start of the Battle of Kara Urgan in Armenia.

9 January Turkish offensive in the Caucasus ends in failure.

10 January Russian troops outflank Turkish *XI Corps* during Kara Urgan battle.

12 January Russians capture several villages near Rosog in East Prussia.

13 January Russians advance on Lower Vistula and occupy Serpets north of Plotsk.

15 January Kara Urgan battle ends. Russians have taken 4,000 Turkish prisoners.

16 January Russians continue to advance on the Lower Vistula, repulsing heavy attacks near Bolimov on the River Ravka, and occupy the Kirlibaba Pass in the Bukovina. Turkish army in Armenia in retreat; its *Third Army* is estimated to have suffered eighty-six per cent losses in just four weeks.

18 January Russian Fifth Army HQ at Mogilnitsa in Poland bombed by a German aircraft. Russians push Turks back towards the border.

20 January Russians take Skempe in north west Poland, advance in the Bukovina, and repulse Austrian attacks on the Kirlibaba Pass.

21 January Further Austrian attack at the Kirlibaba Pass repulsed.

22 January After having been strongly reinforced, the Austrians recapture Kirlibaba.

23 January Austrian *Third Army* starts its winter offensive in the Carpathians to relieve Przemsyl.

25 January Zeppelin PL19 brought down by Russian AA fire from the Libau forts. Russian advance in the Pillkallen district of East Prussia. Fighting continues in the Carpathians. Russian Tenth Army forming to invade East Prussia from the south.

26 January New German *Tenth Army* formed with four corps for a Masurian Lakes offensive under General Eichhorn. Russian success near the Dukla Pass. German *Südarmee* attacks gain very little ground.

27 January Russian counter-attack against *Südarmee*.

28 January *Südarmee* resists Russian counter-attacks and drives them back near Beskid Pass.

29 January Continued heavy fighting between Dukla and Wyszkov Passes with the Russians losing ground. In East Prussia Russians advance towards Tilsit.

30 January German offensive near Lipno in north west Poland is driven back.

31 January Determined German attacks in region of Bolimov gain a little ground. This was the first use of poison gas but it had no effect due to the East wind and intense cold. Russians did not tell their allies about it.

1 February Heavy artillery fire near Riga. *Ninth Army* initially successful on a six-mile front but Russian reserves retake any losses and stabilise the front near Bolimow in Poland. Heavy losses on both sides. In the Carpathians the Russians advance from Dukla pass to Upper San, advance near Uzsok Pass but evacuate Tucholka and Beskid passes.

2 February Severe cold in the Carpathian mountains causes large numbers of frostbite casualties: one Austrian regiment loses over 1,800 men in the night.

3 February Continued desperate fighting on Ravka near Bolimov. Russians storm Skempe in the north west of Poland.

4 February The heavy fighting on Bzura-Ravka front continues with the Russians crossing the Bzura and taking positions near Dachova. In the Bukovina, German pressure forces the Russians back.

5 February Continuous fighting in the Carpathians with Austrian attacks repulsed with heavy losses. Further Russian successes on Bzura and Ravka.

6 February Austrian *Seventh Army* retakes Kimpolung.

7 February German offensive on southern wing of East Prussian front – the Winter Battle of Masuria - is hampered by snow but troops advance 40 kilometres towards Johannisburg in two days. Austrians reach Upper Suczava valley, Bukovina, but in the Carpathians German efforts near Tucholka Pass are repulsed.

8 February Germans take Johannisburg and the Austrians continue to advance in Bukovina.

9 February Austrians advance from Kimpolung. An infantry corps from Serbia reinforces the Austrian front in the Carpathians. Germans take Biala and turn Russian right flank near Pillkallen. Russians withdraw beyond the Suczava. In Galicia, Russian shelling begins the siege of Przemsyl.

10 February German line reaches line Pillkallen-Vladislavov, captures Eydtkuhnen and Wirballen, takes 10,000 POWs and cuts the Russian line of retreat.

11 February Continued Austrian pressure forces the Russians back to the River Sereth. Germans take Serpets in north west Poland but are repulsed at Kosziowa.

12 February Russian cavalry raid Khorzel in East Prussia. Austrians cross the Jablonitsa pass in the Carpathians.

13 February Germans take Russian positions before Lyck. Fierce fluctuating struggle in Carpathians.

14 February Germans take Lyck and 5,000 POWs. There are now no Russian troops left in East Prussia. Russians hold their ground in western Carpathians, but Austrians take Nadworna in East Galicia.

15 February Germans occupy Plotsk.

17 February Russians defeated on line Plotsk-Ratsionj in north west Poland. *XXI.Korps* has 70,000 Russians enveloped in Augustow Forest. Germans attack Przasnysz fortress. Austrians retake Czernowitz. Great battle near Nadworna and Kolomea.

18 February Austrians offensive near Tarnow. Germans take Tauroggen, north east of Tilsit.

19 February Russians check Austrian attack on River Dunajec near Tarnow but retreat near Nadworna. Russian counter-offensive on East Prussian frontier. Austrians retake Stanislau.

20 February Russian Twelfth Army counter-attack near Plotsk is repulsed. German attacks at Kosziowa repulsed.

21 February Successful Russian counter-attacks near Lomja and Plotsk. Russians carry heights near Lupkow and Wyzskow Passes, and make successful attack on Austrians south-east of Stanislau. After attempting to break out of encirclement in Augustow Forest, the Russian XX Corps surrenders. In Armenia Russians drive the Turks across the River Ichkalen.

22 February Masurian Lakes battle ends with Russian losses including 100,000 POWs. South of Dolina-Stanislau in Galicia, a battle begins. Heavy fighting at many points in northern Poland, especially near Przasnysz, where strong German attacks are repulsed.

23 February Russians advance across the Bobr, south-east of Augustovo.

24 February Germans cross the Niemen river near Sventsiansk and take Przasnysz with 10,000 POWs. Russians take Mozely, near Bolimov.

25 February Germans bombard Osovyets fortress for two days. Russians retake Stanislau. Continued heavy fighting near Przasnysz; Russians take 2,600 prisoners.

27 February Russians retake Przasnysz with over 5,000 POWs and claim to have taken 4,000 POWs at Dolina-Stanislau. Early thaw slows down renewed Austrian offensive in the Carpathians; it gains only ten miles by 5 March.

28 February Russians counter-attack Austrians in Galicia.

1 March On the Niemen River front, the German offensive collapses with signs of a general retreat. Heavy fighting near Grodno and Osovyets when Russian Tenth Army counter-attacks. Austrian attacks repulsed in the Carpathians but Hungarians hold Uzsok Pass although ordered to evacuate three times.

2 March Russians bombard Czernowitz. Austrian attacks repulsed at Lupkow Pass. Continued heavy fighting near Grodno and Osovyets. Russian offensive on the Niemen river continues, taking many prisoners.

3 March Russians retake Stanislau and village of Krasna and over 6,000 prisoners. Austrian attacks repulsed in the Carpathians.

4 March Continued fierce Austrian attacks in the Carpathians.

5 March Germans concentrate strong forces between Thorn and Mlava. Russians cross the Bistritza river in the eastern Carpathians and threaten Austrian flank.

6 March Austrians retreat in the Bukovina and their attacks in the Carpathians are repulsed again. *Tenth Army* withdraws from Augustow Forest with Russians in pursuit.

7 March Russians continue their pursuit of the retreating Germans in Augustovo Woods. Heavy fighting at Osovyets. Further Austrian attacks repulsed at Baligrod in the Carpathians.

8 March Despite heavy losses, Austrians continue to attack at Baligrod. Russians checked at Kosziowa (southern Carpathians), but retain positions by a counter-attack. Severe fighting on whole front north of Vistula. Russians make progress at Osovyets.

9 March *Eleventh Army* formed with General der Infantarie von Fabeck in command. New German offensive near Przasnysz in Poland. Russian advance north of Osovyets. Austrian attack fails in the Carpathians. Heavy artillery firing along the river Narev.

10 March Russians repulse renewed German attacks on the Niemen and west of Grodno.

11 March German offensive near Przasnysz makes progress. Russian attack in the Carpathians breaks the Austrian *Second Army* left flank.

12 March Russians repulse German attacks near Augustovo Woods and north of Przasnysz.

13 March Austrian attacks fail in the Carpathians and East Galicia. German offensive checked near the Augustovo Woods and Przasnysz. Russians storm part of the Przemysl perimeter.

14 March Further Russian success in the district of Przasnysz.

15 March Austrian centre broken by Russian counter-offensive near Smolnik in the Carpathians. Russian counter offensive along both banks of the Orzec in northern Poland.

17 March Austrians try to cross the river Pruth in Bukovina. Russians capture and burn Memel.

19 March Austrian sortie from Przemysl fails.

20 March Russians attack Przemysl from three sides. Russians attack, taking 2,400 prisoners, near Smolnik. Russians take Laugszargen in East Prussia and attack Tilsit. *Südarmee* starts attacking near Kosziowa.

21 March Germans retake Memel. Germans abandon attack on Osovyets and withdraw their artillery.

22 March Austrian fortress of Przemysl surrenders. Russians capture over 100,000 POWs including nine generals. Garrison had three days' rations left. Many were ill with scurvy.

23 March Germans retake Tilsit.

25 March Russian counter-offensive makes progress in the Carpathians with 5,700 prisoners taken.

26 March Russians retake Lupkow Pass with over 2,500 POWs reported.

27 March *Südarmee* attacks near Kosziowa cease. Russians repulse German attacks in the Niemen district.

28 March To bolster the Austrians in the Carpathians, the Germans provided *XXXVIII.Korps*, known as the *Beskidenkorps (Beskids Korps:* Beskids being an area in the mountains where it was stationed). Failure of Austrian attacks and progress by Russians in the Carpathians. Attempted renewal of offensive by Germans in northern Poland.

29 March Germans take Tauroggen, north-east of Tilsit. Further Russian advance in the Carpathians; 5,600 prisoners.

31 March Germans bombard Libau. Severe fighting in the Carpathians.

1 April Russians make progress in the Carpathians but their advance in Western Poland is checked. Russian cavalry defeat German cavalry in north Poland. Russians occupy Tsria in Armenia and defeat Turkish army at Oltu.

2 April Russians take Cigielka in the Carpathians and their cavalry defeat German cavalry in north Poland. Fighting continues in the Bukovina but now no Austrians in Russia.

3 April Severe fighting north of Czernowitz. Russian attacks repulsed in the Carpathians.

4 April After two days of snowstorms the Russians reach Sztropko in Hungary and occupy Cisna. Russian hospital bombed at Radom in Poland. Fierce battle at Okna, near Czernowitz.

5 April Austrians want peace with Russia so they can fight against Italy. Russians continue to make progress in the Carpathians.

6 April Russian advance in the Niemen border district. The Beskidenkorps counter-offensive takes Hill 992 in the Carpathians with 6,000 POWs.

7 April Further Russian advance in Carpathians.

9 April Continued fighting in the Carpathians, with Russians resuming their advance and, by 14 April, having taken the mountain crests on a line from the Dukla to Ozsok Pass.

10 April Spring thaw halts part of the Russian Carpathian offensive. Severe fighting for the Uzsok Pass.

11 April Russians capture Wysocko Nizhne, near the Uzsok Pass. Germans bombard Osovyets.

12 April Russians checked east of the Uzsok Pass.

13 April Russians capture heights near Uzsok Pass.

14 April Germans repulsed before Osovyets. Russians make progress east of Czernowitz. Indecisive fighting at the Uzsok Pass.

15 April Eight German Western Front divisions ordered to move east for new attack.

16 April Russians capture two heights south-west of Rosztoki Pass in the Carpathians.

17 April Austrian offensive towards Stryj in eastern Galicia. As a result of the surrender of Dukla Pass to the Russians, *28 Infantry Regiment* (Czech-Austrian) is dissolved.

18 April Russians repulse attacks in the Carpathians.

20 April Austrians repulsed near Gorlice. As a result of the Armenian uprising, Turks besiege Van which is held by Armenian soldiers.

21 April In continued fighting in the Carpathians, the Russians take Height 1002 north-east of Lubonia.

22 April Russian attacks repulsed on both sides of the Uzsok Pass. Austrian attack towards Stryj fails.

24 April Austrians capture Ostaij, a height south-east of Kosziowa.

25 April Severe fighting near Stryj.

27 April German advance towards Shavli in Lithuania. In the Carpathians Russian cavalry beat Austrian *Seventh Army* at Gorodenko.

28 April Austro-German offensive under von Mackensen begins between the Dunajec and Biala Rivers in west Galicia, driving the Russians back.

29 April Russians repulse Austrian attacks in the Uzsok Pass. Continued German advance in Galicia and in the Baltic Provinces where the Libau-Dvinsk railway was reached.

30 April Germans reach the railway stations of the Muravievo and Radziviliski - Province of Kovno in Lithuania.

1 May Germans occupy Shavli and approach Libau. Austro-German attack towards the Uzsok Pass in the Carpathians and the start of an offensive against Gorlice in Galicia.

2 May Austro-Germans take Gorlice and Ciezkowica and cross the Biala. Russians take Mt. Makovoka (near Stryj), but lose it again.

3 May Austro-German offensive in Galicia opens a twelve-mile gap in the Russian line allowing attackers to advance eight miles. They also continue to make progress in the Carpathians and the Baltic where they report having taken over 8,000 POWs during the advance on Mitau.

4 May Severe fighting in Galicia with the Russians making a stand on the Visloka River.

5 May Germans bombard Grodno and are held south of Mitau.

6 May Austrians occupy Tarnow and in the Carpathians a Russian division surrenders to them. Russians launch an offensive through Tortum Valley towards Erzurum in Armenia.

7 May Russians fall back to the Vistok, and blow up Lupkow Pass tunnel during their retreat in the Carpathians.

8 May Severe Russian casualties during a counter-attack near Dukla Pass. Germans take Libau. Further Russian retreat in Galicia.

9 May German forces beaten at Krakinow.

10 May German retreat in Baltic Provinces.

11 May Germans evacuate Shavli in the Baltic Provinces. Austro-German advance in Galicia. Russians fall back to the San River. Russian diversionary offensive across the Dniester, in the Bukovina, takes Nadworna and about 20,000 POWs.

12 May Germans occupy Kyeltsi in Poland. Austrian retreat south of Pruth but advance in Galicia and north of Uzsok Pass.

13 May Russians occupy Sniatyn near the River Pruth but retreat in Galicia.

14 May Battle of the San: Austro-Germans take Jaroslav. Russians take Kolomea.

15 May Russian left drives the Austrians on the Dniester. Austrians pushed back between Kielce and Ostrovyets.

16 May Severe Austrian defeat between Kyeltsi and Ostrovyets in southern Poland. Austro-German forces cross the river San.

17 May Austro-Germans cross the San. Russian troops enter Van in Armenia.

18 May Galician oilfields north east of Uzsok re-occupied by the Austrians. Russians driven from Sieniawa on the River San by Austrian forces.

19 May Germans take Lutkow in Galicia. Mackensen's forces reduce the Russian salient at west of the San.

20 May Von Mackensen forces bombard Russian garrison in Przemsyl. Three Russian corps attack Austrian *Fourth Army*.

21 May Russian evacuate Przemysl under cover of a counter-attack. Austrian *VII.Korps* leaves for the Italian Front.

24 May Austro-Germans occupy Radyno in Galicia. German offensive in Galicia is resumed. *Südarmee* making some progress in Battle of Stryj. Russian offensive towards Erzurum halted by Turks.

25 May Offensive has advanced to eleven miles east of the San taking over 20,000 POWs and the bridgehead of Zagrody on the San.

26 May *Niemenarmee* formed in the Baltic Provinces from *Armee-Gruppe Lauenstein*. Austro-Germans gain successes in severe fighting round Przemsyl.

27 May Russian losses very heavy during the retaking of Sieniawa in Galicia. In the Baltic Provinces Russians take Kindowary near Shavli.

28 May Russians take Bubie in the Baltic Provinces. Austro-German advance on Przemsyl continues.

29 May Russian counter-offensive forces Austrians to retreat in east Galicia.

30 May Austro-Germans shell Przemysl. Russian success on the San.

31 May Austro-Germans capture Stryj and the three northern fronts of Przemsyl.

1 June Unsuccessful German gas attack west of Warsaw.

2 June Austrians beaten on the Dniester at Mikolajow. Austro-German attack on Przemsyl breaks in on two front.

3 June Austro-Germans retake Przemsyl. Large numbers of troops sent to the Italian Front.

4 June Russians cease attacks in Galicia.

6 June *Südarmee* crosses the Dniester at Zurawno, and continues its advance east of Przemsyl.

7 June Russians evacuate Kalusz and Nadworna in east Galicia.

8 June Austrians retake Stanislau.

9 June Russians retake Zurawno. German attacks repulsed in the Shavli district. Austro-Germans pressed back to right of the Dniester.

10 June Turks win second battle of Tortum.

11 June Germans retake Zurawno.

12 June Russians evacuate all of the Bukovina and Austrians retake Kolomea in Galicia. Germans attack north of Shavli, north of Przasnysz, on the Bzura – using gas, and at Mosciska in Galicia.

13 June Germans resume offensive in Galicia on a thirty-one mile front. Russians start retiring towards the Grodek Line near Lemberg. Russian counter-attack on the Styr and Tysmienice.

15 June German advance on right bank of San.

16 June Start of the Third Battle of Lemberg: both sides roughly equal in size. Fighting continues east of the San.

17 June Russians announce German losses of around 120,000 on Dniester during the last month, with 40,000 POWs. As a result of the heavy Russian losses since start of the war STAVKA sanctions a fighting retreat for all Russian armies.

19 June Austro-Germans' attack on the Grodek line in Galicia causes a Russian retreat with the loss of Zolkiew and Rawaruska two days later. Russian forces launch an offensive towards Muş west of Van.

20 June Armenians and Cossacks take Sevan on Lake Van.

21 June Austrians repulsed at Nizniow on the Dniester.

22 June Austrian *Second Army* retakes Lemberg.

23 June Austro-Germans checked on the Zurawno-Demeszknowiec line - Dniester front.

25 June Russians fight a rearguard action at Bobrka. Armenians and Cossacks take Sorp near Lake Van.

26 June German attacks on the Bukaczowce-Halicz front repulsed but others successful with Russians in retreat.

27 June Russians retreat from the line of the Dniester to Gnila-Lipa line. *Südarmee* occupies Halicz and Feldmarschall Mackensen's troops advance to the River Bug. Russian attacks break down north of Przasnysz.

28 June Continued Russian retreat in Galicia.

29 June Mackensen's army continues its advance towards the Vistula and the Bug. Russians repulse an attack near Halicz.

30 June Germans cross Gnila Lipa line. Tomaszow in Poland reached by Feldmarschall Mackensen. Germans claim 150,650 prisoners in June.

1 July Russians evacuate bridgehead near Tarlov on the Vistula front. General von Linsingen's troops cross the Gnila Lipa south of Rohatyn in Galicia and Mackensen's forces occupy Zamosc fortress near the Upper Bug. German cavalry sword officially withdrawn and lance now the sole shock weapon.

2 July Archduke Josef Ferdinand's forces occupy Krasnik. Heavy Austro-Russian engagements between Vistula and Bug.

3 July Russians retreat from Gnila Lipa for Zlota Lipa.

4 July *Südarmee* reaches the Zlota Lipa. General von Linsingen leaves to take command of the new *Bugarmee* and is replaced by Count Bothmer.

5 July Russians inflict serious defeat on Germans between the Vistula and Bug, and their offensive between Veprj and Bug is repulsed. Northern movement of Austro-Germans from Galicia towards Cholm-Lyublin line suspended.

6 July German *Ninth Army* attack on River Bzura fails. Austrian forces beaten near Krasnik with Russians taking 150,000 POWs.

7 July Von Mackensen's army held up near Krasnostav.

8 July Austrians withdraw to heights north of Krasnik after defeat at Urzedowka.

9 July *Südarmee* repulsed on Zlota Lipa.

10 July Austrians counter-attack on Krasnik. Start of the Battle of Mazalgirt in Armenia.

11 July Austro-German attacks on Zlota Lipa and Dniester repulsed. Russians withdraw to right bank of Urzedowka. Fighting on Lyublin front continues; Austrians lose nearly all ground gained in past week.

12 July German offensive on the Bobr and Narev fronts, north-east of Warsaw.

13 July Austrian advance across Dniester in Bukovina and German *Twelfth Army* attack on Narev.

14 July Great Austro-German offensive from Baltic to Bukovina begins. Germans capture Przasnysz as Russians fall back towards Narev. *Bugarmee* involved in local battles for the remainder of the month.

15 July Battles at Sokal and Krasnostav in Poland. *Niemenarmee* advances towards Riga. Germans storm line south of Zielovna near Przasnysz, and force Russians to retreat towards the Narev.

16 July Between Vistula and Bug, Germans attack Russians on the Wolitsa, and the Russians repulse Austrians north of Krasnik.

17 July *Twelfth Army* has advanced five miles on a twenty-five-mile front since 13 July. Mackensen continues offensive on the Wolitsa.

18 July *Niemenarmee* takes Windau in the Baltic Provinces. Russian Guard and Prussian Guard fight for the first time. General Russian retreat sanctioned. Von Mackensen's force takes Krasnostav with 15,000 POWs. Russians retreat from north and west of Warsaw and on entire front of Vistula and Bug.

19 July Germans attacking north and south of Warsaw. Fierce fighting on Lyublin-Cholm line.

20 July Russian counter-attack delays German advance. Austrians occupy Radom. General Woyrsch's troops besiege the Russian garrison of Ivangorod. Terek Cossacks rout a German Infantry Regiment in a moonlight charge. Germans break through Russian line on the Bubissa. Russians evacuate positions west of Groitsi and retreat north of Novogorod - Warsaw region. Stubborn Russian defence of Lyublin-Cholm railway.

21 July Russian offensive round Sokal forces Austro-Germans from right bank of Upper Bug.

22 July Germans storm Miluny near Warsaw and attack the Narev bridgehead at Rojan to the northeast of Warsaw. Russian forces cleared from left bank of Vistula above Ivangorod.

23 July *Niemenarmee* takes Shavli in Courland. General Gallwitz storms Russian positions at Rozan and Pultusk fortress bridgeheads and crosses the Narev river over the next two days.

24 July Russian 1 Cavalry Division checks German advance south of Mitau in the Baltic provinces.

25 July Russians evacuate Riga and Warsaw factories. German troops cross Narev above Ostrolenka and reach Posvol and Poneviezh district on the Dvina.

26 July *Niemenarmee* repulsed at Shlok on the Gulf of Riga. Russian forces aided by warships' guns. Russian attempt to take Muş fails. Turkish forces repulse Russians from Malazgirt and back to their initial line.

27 July Gallwitz's troops take Goworowo and hold against Russian counter-attacks. Russian forces in Warsaw attacked on three sides. Fighting for the Pruth south-east of Poltusk proceeding. Austrians lose heavily in attack near Majdan-Ostrowski and on front Terriatin-Annopol on the Cholm front.

28 July Austrians repulsed beyond the Kamienka on the Upper Vistula. Russians repulsed south-west of Gora Kalvariya near Warsaw. Germans cross Vistula between Warsaw and Ivangorod.

29 July In the Battle of Biskupice, Von Mackensen's troops cut the Lublin-Cholm railway. German troops break through Russian positions west of the Veprj. Unsuccessful German attempt to advance between Narev and the Orz.

30 July Russians fall back along entire line, only resisting north of Grusbieszow on the lower Bug. Evacuation of Warsaw continues and Austrians occupy Lublin.

31 July *Niemenarmee* crosses the River Aa. Russians evacuate Lublin and Cholm. After desperate fighting Germans advance on Kamienka front.

1 August Mitau near Riga evacuated, and captured by Germans. Russians hold Germans on the Blonie line, west of Warsaw but they make progress on the Narev. Austrians capture Novo Alexandria station in Ivangorod and Gallwitz's force captures Ostrolenka.

2 August Russians retreat east of Ponevyej near Dvinsk in Latvia. Germans claim 9,000 prisoners taken near Lomja on the east bank of Vistula. At Ivangorod on the Leczna-Cholm line the Russians lose 2,000 prisoners and evacuate their positions. Advancing Turkish troops occupy Karakilise.

3 August Russians retire north of Lomja and the Germans cross Narev. Mackensen victorious near Cholm. Austrian *First Army* cavalry enters Vladimir Volinski.

4 August Germans threaten Warsaw and civilians are evacuated. The Blonie-Nadarzyn Line, 15 miles west of Warsaw, is abandoned by the Russians. Latter evacuate Ivangorod. Russians outflank Turkish troops near Karakilise.

5 August German troops enter Warsaw and *Tenth Army* attacks Kovno. Austrian *Fourth Army* starts Battle of Lubartow, north of Lublin.

6 August Archduke Joseph Frederick enters Lyublin. Germans repulsed at Osovyets after failed gas attack. Cossacks re-occupy Karakilise.

7 August Russians repulse Germans near Riga but they reach the Vistula near Pienkow in Poland. Germans attack Kovno and Russians retreat behind the Jara river. German attack near Osovyets with gas. Sierok (northern Georgievsk) occupied by German troops. Russian night attack forces Turkish troops to retreat from Mirgemir Pass.

8 August Russians repulse attacks on Kovno. Austrian victory at Battle of Lubartow. Germans occupy Warsaw Praga suburb. Russians in Novo Georgievsk fortress cut off. Start of the Battle of Ostrov. Mackensen forces Russians back across the Veprj.

9 August Gallwitz's force takes Lomja in Poland. After a night attack on Kovno fortress Germans lose three battalions in the Russian counter-attack. Germans advance east of Warsaw. Osovyets evacuated and destroyed by Russians.

10 August Siege of Novo Georgievsk under General von Beseler, and Brest-Litovsk bombarded. Russians dislodged north-west of Kock and Germans reach Kaluszyn, east of Warsaw. Lomja and Ostrov taken by the Germans. Vilna and Kovno being evacuated.

11 August Russians evacuate Dvinsk.

12 August Russians retake Kovarsk and Toviamy but evacuate Lukow, Sokolov, and Syedlets during their retreat from Warsaw. Austro-German armies in touch west of Brest-Litovsk and form unbroken line. Germans driven back beyond Aa, south-west of Mitau.

13 August *Bugarmee* repulsed after three days' fighting from Vlodava on the Upper Bug.

14 August Russians attack near Czernowitz (Bukovina) but their sortie from Kovno is repulsed. Germans force crossing on the river Nurzec.

15 August 1,730 Russians taken prisoners outside Kovno. Losice, Biala, and Mazyrecze, west of Brest, are captured. Germans cross the Bug river east of Droghiczyn. Russian line broken at Bransk on the river Nurzec with the loss of 5,000 prisoners.

16 August Austrians cross the Krzna Brest. Bombardment of Kovno breaches its defences. Russian army withdraws to the Brest-Osovyets-Kovno line. Byelostok (Grodno) partially evacuated by the Russians.

17 August German assault on Novo-Georgievsk captures the outlying forts. Austrians approach Brest-Litovsk. Russians driven across Bug at Konstantinov.

19 August Russians driven back between Augustovo and Osovyets. Germans progress beyond the Niemen river east of Tykocin. Mackensen reaches Piszcza and gains ground towards Brest-Litovsk. Attempted landing at Pernau in the Gulf of Riga fails. Austrian cavalry advances on Kovel. General Gallwitz's troops fighting the Battle of Bielsk.

20 August Fall of Novo Georgievsk with the loss of 90,000 POWs including thirty generals. Russians evacuate Byelostok and Germans occupy Byelsk, north of Brest.

21 August In East Prussia, Second Army under Samsonov advances and occupies, between August 21 and 23, Allenstein, Neidenburg, Soldau and Johannisburg.

22 August Austrian *Fourth Army* takes Kovel and Russians fall back from the Bobr and Niemen rivers. Osovyets falls to Austrians after Russians evacuate and blow up defences. In Poland the Russians evacuate Kyeltsi.

23 August Germans evacuate Insterburg in East Prussia and are driven back at the Battle of Frankenau. In Galicia the Russians take Brody and Tarnopol.

24 August Austrians break through advanced position near Dobrynka .

25 August *Bugarmee* occupies Brest-Litovsk during its advance north.

26 August *Twelfth Army* under Gallwitz occupies Bialystok. General Eichhorn's *Tenth Army* occupies Fort Olita on the Niemen river and is ordered to advance on Vilna the next day. Start of Austrian 'Black Yellow Offensive'.

27 August Russian line on Zlota Lipa broken near Brzezany.

28 August *Tenth Army* ordered to advance on Vilna in the Baltic Provinces.

29 August Friedrichstadt bridgehead in the Baltic Provinces taken by the *Niemenarmee*. German advance approaches Grodno and Vilna. Lipsk north west of Grodno stormed and the Sidra section to the south is evacuated.

30 August Russian victory on Strypa in southern Galicia, taking 4,000 prisoners and thirty guns.

31 August In the Pripet region, the Austrian *First Army* takes Lutsk with 7,000 POWs. Germans reach Orani near Vilna.

1 September With the German *Tenth Army* only 30 km from Vilna the Russians concentrate troops for the city's defence. The German *Eighth Army* storms the fortress at Grodno.

2 September Grodno falls to German attacks. General von Boehm-Ermolli's army advances east of Brody. Russians retreat to the Sereth and there is fierce fighting near Vilna.

3 September Germans force Russians at Friedrichstadt on to the east bank of Dvina. Russians re-enter Grodno and hold a line between Dniester and Pripet marshes. General von Beseler appointed Governor General of Russian Poland.

4 September First day of the Battle of Drohiczyn-Chomet which lasts until 6 September.

5 September Fighting on Styr and Sereth rivers.

6 September Russians pressed back in centre by Germans and over the east Galician border by Austrians. Heavy fighting near Brody.

7 September The Austrians enter Dubno but to the south there is a successful Russian-counter-offensive on the Sereth at Tarnopol and Trembovia. Germans take Volkovisk.

8 September Russian victory at Tarnopol and Trembovia with 8,000 prisoners taken.

9 September Russians hold their own in north and return to their former positions on the Sereth taking 5,000 more prisoners. Vilna offensive starts.

10 September Russian success continues in southern Galicia. German attacks north of Vilna.

11 September German offensive towards Minsk forces Russian III Siberian Corps to retreat to cover the city. Austrians retreat towards the River Strypa.

12 September German cavalry cut the Vilna-Riga railway taking Sventsyani. Russians pressed back east of Grodno.

13 September At the Battle of Slonim, the Austro-German forces are held. Desperate fighting from the Dvina to the Vilia river, and a vigorous German offensive towards Dvinsk - the Battle of Meiszagola.

14 September *I Cavalry Division* occupies Smorgon on the Vilna-Minsk railway. Continued pressure by German forces in the northern sector. Russians successful in Rovno and Tarnopol districts.

15 September German cavalry occupy Vileika and Krivichi, east of Vilna. Austrians driven back across Strypa in the south. Fighting west and south of Dvinsk with the Germans aiming to divide the Russian Vilna and Dvinsk groups.

16 September *Bugarmee* occupies Pinsk in the Pripet region. Russian position on the Vilna-Dvinsk front is critical but Russians continue to hold on.

17 September Austrian *Fourth Army* checked west of Rovno. Russian positions on the Vilna and Dvinsk front are dangerously threatened so Russians retire between Vilia and Pripet Rivers.

18 September Infantry reinforce German cavalry in Vileika and Krivichi. Vilna falls to *Tenth Army* and the Russians retreat towards Minsk. Austro-Germans retire in Rovno region.

19 September Russians re-occupy Smorgon. Germans reach Smorgon and Molodechna - between Vilna and Minsk. Russians make a stand on Upper Vilia river.

20 September Heavy fighting near Riga.

21 September Tough fighting near Dvinsk. Russians re-occupy Smorgon. Further Austrian withdrawals in the Rovno region.

22 September General von Fabeck replaces General von Gallwitz as commander of *Twelfth Army*. Successful Russian operations along whole line except in the centre.

23 September Russian 4 Division retakes Lutsk with 12,000 POWs. Germans driven back across Oginski Canal at Pinsk. Russians recapture Vileika on the Minsk Front.

25 September South of Dvinsk the Russians retake Drisviati and attacking German forces are driven back with severe losses.

26 September *Bugarmee* crosses the River Styr. Ludendorff orders the building of the Dauerstellung (permanent position) Line. Fighting round Dvinsk continues. South of Pinsk German troops driven back.

27 September Russians defeat *Niemenarmee* at Eckau and retake Vileika and Krivichi. Russian Twelfth Army retreats to the River Dvina.

28 September *Bugarmee* repulsed north of Pinsk but Russians abandon Lutsk. Germans press Russians back in Pripet district but lose heavily in marshes.

29 September *Niemenarmee* becomes new *Eighth Army*. Severe fighting south-east of Dvinsk and on Strypa in Galicia. Russians driven back in Pripet region.

30 September German advance comes to a standstill nearly all along line, though Russians still retiring slowly round Lutsk and in Southern Pripet marshes region.

1 October German attacks on Dvinsk and Smorgon and Linsingen's force gains ground 25 miles east of Lutsk.

2 October Battle of Vilna ends.

3 October Desperate fighting in Lake region south of Dvinsk. The Russian offensive between Postavi and Smorgon collapses.

4 October Russians take the offensive between Drisviati Lake and Smorgon.

5 October Riga front active and continued fighting near Smorgon.

6 October Heavy fighting on the Dvina front and in the Lakes district

7 October Russian offensive started on 2 October fails. Fighting continues in the Dvinsk region.

8 October Russians capture 1,000 prisoners at Novo Alexinatz on the Galician border, east of Lemberg.

9 October Russians pressed back north-west of Dvinsk and south-west of Pinsk, taking heavy losses in Volhynia.

10 October Scattered fighting along most of the line, except Dvinsk where Russians are forced back.

11 October Desperate fighting near Dvinsk. In Galicia Ivanov captures 2,000 Austrians on River Strypa in Galicia. Russians repulse Turkish attack at Ichkau.

12 October Fighting continues in the Dvinsk region. Russians take Visniovtchyk but are driven back over the River Strypa. Turkish attacks at Van Pass and Arkhava repulsed by Russians.

13 October Russians hold their own at Lake Drisviati near Dvinsk.

14 October Germans cross River Eckau near Mitau. Violent fighting at Illukst near Dvina.

16 October Heavy fighting along Russian front, specially near Mitau.

17 October *Eighth Army* active near Jakobstadt. Russians successful on middle Styr and attack south of Dvinsk.

18 October Germans advance on the Dvina and Russian 4 Division captures Chartorysk on the River Styr from *14 Division*.

19 October *Eighth Army* active near Mitau. Russians successful on the River Styr.

20 October Russians take 7,500 prisoners near Tarnopol.

21 October Fighting at Baranovichi, northern Polesia, with the Russians taking 3,500 POWs. Germans capture Dvina bank ten miles east of Riga. In Galicia the Austrian *Second Army* holds the Russian Eleventh Army at the Battle of Novo Alexinatz.

22 October Germans take Kolki to west of Chartorysk. In the Gulf of Riga, Russian Landing Party repulses German forces near Dömesnes.

23 October Further Russian attacks south of Dvinsk. Fighting begins on the Oginski Canal north of Pinsk. Germans storm Illukst.

24 October Germans repulsed on Lower Aa near Riga but take Dahlen Island near Riga.

25 October Furious fighting near Illukst, Üxküll, Lake district and Chartorysk in the Baltic Provinces.

26 October Germans advance past Illukst.

27 October Indecisive fighting on most of the front except on the River Styr where the Russians are driven back.

28 October *Army Detachment Scholtz* (previously *Armee-Gruppe Scholtz*) formed. German forces concentrating near Riga with fierce fighting on Dvina river.

30 October Russians claim thousands of prisoners near Tarnopol and the Germans claim 3,000. *Südarmee* fighting the Battle of Siemeikowice.

1 November The Battle of Dvinsk ends in stalemate.

3 November Russians take 5,000 Austrian POWs after Strypa boat crossing and defeat Germans at Siemeikowice.

5 November Russians repulse German attack at Platonovka, south of Sventen.

6 November With naval support, Russian counter-attack retakes Olai south of Riga.

7 November Russians make progress near Riga.

9 November In the Pripet region the Russians break through the German positions near Kolki on the River Styr taking 3,500 POWs.

10 November Russian attacks break German lines west of Chartorysk, taking over 2,000 POWs.

11 November Russians take Kemmern with naval support.

12 November Meeting between Kaiser and Hindenburg. Hindenburg threatens to resign if Kaiser insists on capture of Riga and Dvinsk.

13 November Germans retreat in the Baltic Provinces.

14 November German retreat south-west from Riga and the Shlok and Kemmern regions.

23 November Russians take Tsarzemunde on the Riga front.

24 November Russians turn German left flank by capture of Yarnopol, north of Illukst, forcing the Germans to abandon the salient.

28 November Staff of *82 Division* surprised and taken prisoner by Terek Cossacks near Pinsk; two generals captured.

29 November Successful Russian action at Illukst.

2 December Germans driven back to the left bank of the Styr river in Galicia.

3 December Austrian offensive repulsed at several points in Galicia.

5 December German artillery bombards Russian positions on Dvinsk front. Russian attack near Lake Babit, west of Riga, collapses.

9 December Russian positions west of Riga shelled with gas and explosive.

15 December Russian attacks north of Lake Drisviati near Dvinsk repulsed.

17 December Austrian attacks on the River Styr repulsed.

19 December Russian attacks repelled near mouth of Beresina river.

24 December Heavy fighting on River Strypa.

27 December Russians open a new offensive along a ninety-mile front from the River Prut to north of the Dniester river. Defending Austrian *Seventh Army* repels six attacks on the first day. Heavy Russian losses for little gain.

28 December Latvian troops rout the Germans on the River Aa in Courland.

30 December Heavy fighting in Bukovina continues.

31 December Strong Russian offensive across River Styr at Chartorysk.

1916

1 January Russian offensive on the Strypa and the Styr in Galicia. Indecisive fighting in the Baltic Provinces throughout month.

2 January Heavy fighting north-east of Czernowitz in the Bukovina Region.

3 January Russian offensive developing in Bukovina and eastern Galicia and Poland. Austrian attacks on the Styr repulsed.

7 January In the Pripet region the Russians storm Chartorysk.

8 January Ivanov offensive resumes in Galicia with heavy fighting.

9 January Further Russian offensive in Bukovina.

10 January Start of the Russian winter offensive on Caucasus front. Turkish *Third Army* driven back on Erzerum with heavy losses.

12 January Resumption of Russian offensive in Galicia.

13 January Russian Fifth Army success at Garbonovka.

15 January Russian progress on the Styr, south of Pinsk.

17 January Russian offensive dies down.

18 January Austrians claim complete victory in Galicia and Bukovina.

19 January Renewed activity north-east of Czernowitz.

21 January Russians renew attack in eastern Poland.

25 January Russians seize Kargapazar Ridge near Erzerum.

29 January Renewed fighting on the Strypa and in Bukovina; Austrians claim success.

30 January Another German gas regiment arrives.

1 February Violent shelling south east of Riga.

3 February Russian attack in Bukovina resumed.

7 February Heavy artillery duel round Riga.

8 February Russians reach west bank of Dniester.

9 February Severe fighting in Volhynia and Galicia.

11 February Russians repulsed south of Dvinsk.

13 February Russians take Garbonovka in the Dvinsk region. Severe fighting in Galicia.

14 February Continued Russian success round Dvinsk.

15 February German attacks in Dvinsk district repulsed.

16 February Erzurum in Armenia falls to Russians.

20 January Russian success on the Dniester in Bukovina.

26 February General Linsingen and Archduke Josef Ferdinand promoted Colonel General.

1 March British arrange to supply Russians with gas shells.

3 March Russians push Turks back in several places.

7 March German artillery active south-west of Dahlen Island (River Dvina). Shelling again in the Riga area.

9 March Russians repulse attacks at Cebrow and Dvina.

10 March German attacks repulsed east of Kosloff.

14 March Much artillery activity on Riga front.

16 March Russians take Mamahatun in Armenia with 800 POWs.

17 March Spring thaw begins unexpectedly early but Russians do not postpone offensive.

18 March First battle of Lake Naroch begins with Russians gaining a mile on a two-mile front for 15,000 casualties.

19 March Russian success north-west of Uscieczko (River Dniester) in Galicia.

20 March Across the front 169 Russian divisions face eighty-six Austrian and German ones. In Armenia Cossacks and 39th Division storm Abdalcik and Askale. Tatvan re-captured from the Turks.

21 March Russian offensive on the northern front; Dvina crossed in force near Jakobstadt with limited success. Russian success on River Dniester.

22 March Russian success at Lake Naroch: 1,000 prisoners reported after two German regiments break.

23 March German concentration at Dvinsk broken up.

27 March Russian right wing ceases attacks due to trenches becoming waterlogged.

28 March Russian success north of Bojan (Galicia).

29 March Thaw on the Russian front suspends operations.

30 March Germans driven back over River Oldenevitz.

2 April Germans repulsed in Liakhovichi region.

3 April Germans repulsed at bridgehead of Üxküll (Dvina).

4 April General Brusilov succeeds General Ivanov in command of southern front.

7 April Renewed fighting at Lake Naroch (south of Dvinsk). Hindenburg marks fifty years' military service with a reception at German GHQ at Kovno. Renewed fighting at Lake Naroch (south of Dvinsk).

8 April 5,000 Russians land near Humurgan on the Turkish Black Sea coast.

10 April Celebrating Orthodox Easter, four Russian regiments fraternise with the Austrians who capture over 100.

12 April Germans repulsed near Dvinsk.

14 April End of first battle of Lake Naroch with Russian losses of over 120,000 against German losses of 20,000.

15 April Russians take two lines of trenches near Lake Naroch.

18 April Russian forces capture Trabzon on Black Sea coast.

20 April Russians begin preparations for next offensive.

28 April Germans regain all ground lost at Lake Naroch.

7 May Austrians ignore discovery of four Russian corps between Kolki and Rovno.

14 May 1,000 British POWs arrive at Zeren, near Riga for reprisal tree-felling.

21 May Russian 127 Infantry Division lands at Trabzon on Turkish Black Sea coast.

27 May General Linsingen tells the Kaiser that he is confident that the Russians will not breach his defences. In Galicia Russian cavalry successfully charge Austrian cavalry near Vonchach in Galicia.

29 May Turkish surprise attack against weak I Caucasus Corps retakes Mamahatun.

30 May Kaiser visits Hindenburg at GHQ in Kovno. Russian 123 Infantry Division lands at Trabzon.

1 June Russians repel attack east of Krevo in west Russia and stop Turkish attacks near Erzerum.

3 June Austrians intercept Russian attack message. Russian bombardment in Riga area, Galicia and Volhynia.

4 June Great Russian offensive from Pripet (Poland) to Romanian frontier (200 mile front), under General Brusilov; 13,000 prisoners reported.

5 June In the Pripet region, Russian Eighth Army breaks through Austrian *Fourth Army*: 12,000 prisoners reported. German attacks repulsed near Krevo.

6 June Russians take Lutsk (Volhynia); cross the Ikva and Styr in Lutsk area and make progress south of Dniester: 15,000 prisoners reported.

7 June Russian offensive continues; 11,000 prisoners reported.

8 June Russian offensive continues; 13,000 prisoners reported. Russians repulse attacks in Vilna district. Austrians forced to send two divisions from the Italian Front with a further 1½ to follow.

9 June Russians capture bridgehead at Rojishche (north of Lutsk) and cross the Strypa; 500 prisoners reported.

10 June Falkenhayn, Chief of Staff of the German Army, orders five divisions south to meet the threat and sends four from Verdun. Russians take Dubno (Volhynia); enemy retire from Strypa; heavy fighting on whole front; 3,500 prisoners reported.

11 June Austrians replace commander of their *Fourth Army*. Russians reach suburbs of Czernowitz; repel attacks near Dvinsk and Vilna; are checked at Lutsk and lose ground on Strypa; 7,000 prisoners reported.

12 June Austrians retreat south of Lutsk. Zaleszczycki (Bukovina) taken by Russians.

13 June Russians repulsed at Baranovichi (75 miles north of Pinsk); take Torchin and reach the Stokhod (near Lutsk); gain ground near Czernowitz; 6,000 prisoners reported.

14 June Fighting at Lokachi and Kolki (Lutsk area); 31,000 prisoners reported. *X.Korps* arrives from Verdun. Austrian cavalry plug the gap between their *First* and *Fourth* armies.

15 June Russians advance north-west of Czernowitz; heavy fighting in the centre.

16 June Russians cross Styr and Stokhod north-west of Lutsk; Austrians retreat across Strypa. German counter offensive in Ukraine.

17 June Russians occupy Czernowitz as Austrians retreat to River Sereth; gain ground west of Kolki (Lutsk) and repel attacks near Buczacz. Germans retake Svidniki.

19 June Russians cross Pruth west of Czernowitz; heavy fighting near Lutsk, Germans reinforcing Austrians.

20 June Germans penetrate Russian lines at Smorgon (Vilna), but are driven out; Russians cross Sereth (south of Czernowitz).

21 June Russians occupy Radautz (south of Czernowitz); Germans repulsed in areas of Dvinsk, Vilna and Lutsk; Russians take trenches on Strypa.

22 June Russians repulse attacks west of Minsk; Russians advance in Bukovina.

23 June Russians take Kimpolung (Bukovina); heavy fighting near Pinsk (Pripet); total prisoners reported since 4 June, 144,000, with 4,031 officers and 219 guns.

24 June Russians checked in Lutsk salient; Austrians driven out of Bukovina.

25 June Russian advance from Bukovina; fighting on Dniester. After surprise crossing of the Pontic Alps, Turkish troops overwhelm Russian 19 Turkistani Regiment.

26 June Turkish offensive through Eastern Black Sea mountains with the objective of retaking Trabzon. The attacks are a failure.

27 June Germans repulsed in Riga and Dvinsk areas. Russian advance from Kolomea (Bukovina).

28 June Heavy fighting on Lutsk salient; Austrians defeated on 25-mile front east of Kolomea; 10,000 prisoners reported; Germans repulsed in Riga district.

29 June Germans repulsed north-east of Vilna.

30 June Two Austrian divisions arrive from the Italian Front. Turkish troops after crossing Pontic Alps within fifteen miles of coast road but Russians hold them at Serpent Rock Hill.

1 July At the River Pruth Russians advance north-west of Kolomea. Austro-Germans progress north-west of Tarnopol.

2 July Russian offensive at Smorgon and Baranovichi penetrates German lines. Germans continue advance on Lutsk salient. South of Dniester they regain Tlumacz. End of Turkish attempt to retake Trabzon. Start of Battles of Bayburt and Dumalidag.

3 July Battle of Baranovichi continues south of Vilna. Russian sea-attack on German lines near Riga.

4 July Russians take Austrian frontline during Baranovichi battle after two days' shelling. Russian Third Army crosses River Styr at Kolki and Rafalovka, pushing Linsingen's troops west to River Stokhod. Further south they cut Carpathian railway at Mikolichin.

5 July In Galicia, Russians continue their attacks south of Dniester and on the Riga and Baranovichi fronts.

6 July Between the Styr and Stokhod Germans fall back in disorder from Chartorysk salient.

7 July Russians reach Manevichi station on Kovel-Sarni railway in northern Lutsk salient.

8 July Russians break through north of Lutsk and cross Upper Stokhod at Ugli and Arsenovich, having advanced 25 miles in four days on a 40-mile front. South of Dniester they capture Delatyn and threaten right flank of Bothmer's army. On the Armenia Front Russian attacks force two Turkish corps to retreat.

10 July Germans rally and offer strong resistance on west bank of the Stokhod. Austrians concentrate troops for big offensive on south side of Lutsk salient. Russians claim 300,000 prisoners to date. Responding to General Falkenhayn's demand, Enver Paşa orders Turkish troops to the Eastern Front. Russians retake Mamahatun from Turks.

11 July Germans receive reinforcements and heavy artillery to defend passage of the Stokhod.

12 July Furious fighting continues on the Stokhod, with no decisive results.

13 July Sharp fighting in Austrian centre, north-west of Buczacz, on the Strypa. Fighting at Stokhod indecisive.

14 July End of Battle of Baranovichi with Russian losses of 80,000 against German losses of 16,000.

15 July On the Riga front Russians, supported by sea and land artillery, make slight advance west of Kemmern. Russian troops, on the southern Lutsk salient, anticipating an Austrian offensive (information from agents), attack them on the Upper Styr. Turks evacuate Bayburt and Russians occupy the town.

16 July Sakharov drives Austrians back on to the Lipa, captures Mikhailovka, taking 13,000 prisoners. Russian advance against *Eighth Army* near Riga peters out.

17 July Russians make progress in the Carpathians. Russian forces occupy Bayburt in Turkey.

18 July German seaplanes drop bombs on Reval on the Gulf of Bothnia. Continued Russian pressure against the Austrians drives them south of the Lipa. Russian advance near Bayburt continues. They take 800 prisoners and Gumusane.

20 July Sakharov defeats Austrians on south-west of Lutsk salient; attacks and carries Berestechko. Heavy fighting on Riga front resumed. On the Armenian Front V Caucasus Corps occupies Ardasa.

21 July Russians drive Austro-Germans over the River Styr, taking 14,000 prisoners.

22 July Austrians, retreating before Sakharov, begin to evacuate Brody.

23 July Kuropatkin's troops drive Germans back south-east of Riga. Russians advance 12 miles near Kemmern.

24 July Russians repulse Germans from Üxküll to Riga.

25 July Sakharov again attacks Austrians east of Styr and advances on Brody. Defeats von Linsingen on River Slonuvka: newly arrived Austrian *106 Landsturm Division* fails to stop the Russians. Russian forces occupy Erzincan after routing Turkish *Third Army* and taking 17,000 POWs.

27 July Sakharov reaches Klekotov position, within five miles of Brody.

28 July Sakharov enters Brody, having captured 40,000 prisoners and 49 guns in 12 days. Further north Brusilov offensive resumed, Lesch and Kaledin attacked on Upper Stokhod, crossing river at many points.

30 July In the direction of Kovel and in the region south of the Dniester towards Stanislau, Russians pursue retreating Austrians.

31 July Russian advance on the Stokhod towards Kovel. Heavy engagements. Russians north of Dniester have crossed Koropyets River.

1 August Russian 66 Division captures Ognot on the Armenian Front.

2 August German gas attack in region of Smorgon (east Vilna) repulsed. Hindenburg appointed C-in-C of Eastern Front. On the Armenian Front, in a new Turkish offensive, Kamal's *XVI Corps* attacks Russians at Bitlis and Muş.

3 August Russians penetrate into Rudka-Mirynska (east of Kovel). Desperate fighting near Lyubashevo and Guledichi (east of Kovel). In the Carpathians, Austrian counter-offensive makes few gains.

4 August Russian offensive in Galicia renewed, taking over 8,000 POWs. Fierce fighting in progress on the Graberko and Sereth with Russians taking over 1,000 POWs. Germans regain Rudka-Mirynska.

5 August Turks reoccupy Bitlis and Muş.

6 August Russians gain heights and villages on right bank of Sereth and Graberko (south Brody) and repel German counter-attacks.

7 August Russians capture Tlumacz after gas shell barrage. Over 10,000 Austrian and German POWs taken. Russian advance in Graberko-Sereth region takes 2,000 prisoners.

8 August In the Pripet region, Russian Guard and Third Armies attack make no gains. Russians take Tysmienica (Galicia), with 7,400 prisoners.

9 August Russians gain junction of Chryplin near Stanislau.

10 August Russians take Stanislau and 8,500 prisoners. Russians cross the Sereth and repulse repeated German counter-attacks. Russians cross the Zlota-Lipa and advance on Halicz.

12 August In east Galicia, the *Südarmee* retreat from the Strypa. Russians cross the Zlota-Lipa and occupy Mariampol. 5 Caucasus Rifle Division blocks attack by Turkish *III Corps* at Boran.

13 August German attack repulsed in region of the Stokhod (Volhynia).

14 August Russians press retreating Austrians, Halicz (Galicia) threatened, and continue passage of the Zlota-Lipa.

15 August Another Russian force reaches Zlota-Lipa, south of Brzezany in Galicia, and also Solotwina (west of Stanislau). Russian 6 Caucasus Rifle Division drives Turkish *IV Corps* south of Ognot.

16 August Heavy Russian attacks west of Sereth in Galicia.

17 August Strong German attacks beaten back by Russians on Zlota-Lipa (Galicia) front.

20 August Muş bridge taken by Russian IV Caucasus Corps with 500 POWs.

22 August Russians gain heights south of Jablonica Pass (Carpathians). German attack with gas, south-east of Vilna, repulsed. Two Turkish divisions take over section of the *Südarmee* line in Galicia. First Turkish troops in Galicia are in position and ready for action.

26 August In Galicia the Russians make slight advance towards Halicz.

29 August Russians capture Mount Pantyr, north-west of Jablonica Pass in the Carpathians. Hindenburg appointed as Chief of Staff of the German Army.

31 August Fighting at Halicz and east of Lemberg; many prisoners taken in Lutsk area by Russians. Austrian losses calculated as over 600,000 and German losses at 150,000.

1 September Fresh Russian advance in Volhynia. Turkish *IV Corps* attack initially successful.

2 September First encounter of the Turkish forces in Galicia with the Russians.

3 September Russians capture position near Brzezany taking many prisoners. Russian success near Dorna Vatra in the Carpathians.

4 September On the Zlota Lipa front, General Brusilov's troops successful, 19,000 prisoners within four days. Unsuccessful German gas attacks near Baranovichi in the Carpathians.

5 September Seven miles south-east of Halicz the Russians claim success; many prisoners taken.

7 September Halicz (on the Dniester) on fire, and taken by Russians. Turkish *XV Corps* retreats for ten miles before standing firm.

10 September Austrian front withdrawn west of the Valley of Gyergyo and Czik in the Carpathians. Kirchbach replaces Pflanzer-Baltin as C-in-C of Austrian *Seventh Army*. Russian reinforcements stop Turkish *IV Corps* attacks near Kigi.

11 September Russians capture Mount Capel Kapul in Carpathians taking many prisoners and linking with Romanian Army.

16 September On the Halicz front, Russians capture a position on the right bank of Zlota-Lipa and many prisoners. Along the Narajowka many Germans taken as well as Turks, but Turks hold their positions.

19 September Russian Seventh Army has taken 25,000 POWs in Galicia since 31 August.

20 September On the Stokhod, in severe fighting near the Kovel-Rovno railway, the German attacks are repulsed.

22 September Russians reported about 50 miles from Lemberg.

26 September Turkish "Çoruh Campaign" on the Caucasus front concludes with limited gains at a high cost; *Second Army* has lost 30,000 men since 2 August. Turks evacuate Muş as first snow falls. Early winter quarters for both sides.

30 September Great battle in Galicia (near Zlota-Lipa and Brzezany) commences when III Caucasus Corps attacks Turkish *XV Corps*. Turks lose heavily but regain positions and take 500 Russian POWs.

1 October In region of Brody, Russians advance after severe fighting. Heavy snow forces many Turkish deserters back to their regiments. Number of deserters from Turkish *Third Army* in the order of 50,000.

2 October Around Zlota-Lipa furious fighting continues. Russians take 1,000 prisoners, but front remains unchanged. On the Brody-Zloczow road, Germans claim recapture of all positions lost on 30 September. Start of Russian mutinies with three soldiers shot and six imprisoned.

3 October West of Lutsk (Volhynia), objective Vladimir Volymski, Russians gain some German positions. Northern Army (4th) left wing, 12 miles south-east of Maros Vasarhely, continues to advance.

4 October Battle west of Lutsk still in progress, German troops obstinately hold positions on Zlota-Lipa.

5 October Lutsk battle in progress. Russians renew their attack in Galicia and manage to take a hill at the south part of the Turkish line.

6 October Russian activities removed from Volhynia to northern Galicia; fighting renewed at Brzezany in the Zlota-Lipa region.

9 October East of Brzezany in Galicia, Germans assume offensive, fighting on Volhynia front. German *Twelfth Army* disbanded.

15 October *Südarmee* involved in the Battle of Lower Narajowka.

16 October Powerful artillery fire halts the Russian attack towards Vladimir-Volinski during the last part of the Brusilov offensive.

17 October North of Korytnitsa (24 miles W.S.W. of Lutsk), after obstinate fighting, Germans take the trenches and 1,900 prisoners.

22 October Stiff fighting north of Halicz (Galicia) for river heights.

23 October Germans claim total repulse of Russians from west bank of Narajowka. Battle in Halicz dies down.

27 October Russian centre on the west bank of the Shchara river, near Minsk, is forced to retire to east bank of river by German attacks.

30 October Germans and Turks force back Russians near River Narajowka in Galicia, allowing the Turks to advance towards Lutsk.

31 October Although the Russians repulse German attacks in the Narajowka Valley, they fall back at Mieczysczow.

9 November Defeat of Russian centre at Skrobova with 3,400 prisoners taken.

28 November Russian success in Carpathians, heights east of Jablonitsa Pass taken.

29 November Russians' Carpathian offensive continues.

30 November Russians repulsed on the Zlota Lipa.

1 December Russians driven off Rukida and Kirlibaba heights in the Carpathians.

2 December Russian offensive in Carpathians continues.

3 December Severe fighting in Carpathians.

4 December Fighting in Stanislau and Tarnopol in Galicia. Russians capture peak commanding Jablonitsa Pass.

5 December German counter-attacks in Carpathians.

6 December Fighting in Volhynia, west of Lutsk, round Tarnopol and Stanislau in Galicia and round Dorna Vatra in the Bukovina.

7 December Russians attack in south-east Galicia.

8 December Heavy fighting in Galicia.

10 December Stubborn fighting in the Carpathians.

12 December Fighting continues round Tarnopol and Stanislau in Galicia.

14 December Fighting continues in the Carpathians.

15 December German success on Tarnopol Railway, west of Lutsk.

16 December Russian positions between Kovel and Lutsk captured.

17 December Fighting continues in the Tarnopol region.

18 December Russian positions between Kovel and Lutsk, lost on 16 December, are retaken.

20 December Severe fighting west of Brody in Galicia.

21 December Fighting south of Dvinsk and also on south Galician rivers.

25 December Turks driven south by Russian attacks near Lake Van.

1917

1 January STAVKA orders reduction in divisional size from 16 to 12 battalions, excluding Guard divisions and units on the Armenian front. Aim to form 62 new divisions by mid-March.

2 January In Galicia, *Südarmee* attack near Zloczow is repulsed. In the Baltic provinces General Scholtz takes over *Eighth Army* for General Mudra. General Hutier replaces Scholtz at *Army Detachment D.*

3 January Russians lose Dvina near Dvinsk in the Baltic provinces but regain it a few days later. In the Bukovina an attack near Mt Botosul takes over 2,000 German POWs. Three night attacks on Russian positions fail.

5 January In the Baltic provinces, Russian Twelfth Army offensive to the west of Riga – the Battle of the Aa - without preliminary shelling gains four miles and 8,000 POWs by 11 January despite counterattacks.

23 January *Eighth Army* counter-offensive regains most ground lost near Riga, taking 900 POWs.

1 February In snow-camouflage, troops break through Russian lines south of Halicz and cross Dniester river ice, but both attacks repulsed.

2 February Attacks east of Kalutsem Highroad in the Baltic Provinces, west of Riga, repulsed by Russians.

3 February Battle of the Aa ends.

5 February Attack in the Pripet region repulsed by Russians.

14 February Successful raid against Russian positions between Zloczow and Tarnopol in Galicia.

16 February Evidence indicates to *OHL* that Russia will not last the year.

17 February In the Baltic Provinces, snow-camouflaged troops take 50 POWs on River Lavkassa southwest of Dvinsk.

25 February In the Baltic provinces, British POWs used to dig trenches, often under Russian fire.

1 March Colonel-General Arz succeeds Conrad as Austro-Hungarian Chief of Staff.

2 March Fighting near Riga. Russians pushed back on River Narajowka and counter-attacks fail. The Tsar abdicates.

3 March Russian gas attacks north of Lake Naroch. *I Landwehr Division* attack in the Pripet region, west of Lutsk, takes 9,000 POWs.

8 March Russians repulse attack near Mitau in Baltic and attack to the east using gas.

12 March In Galicia, raids successful against Russian positions near Zlozow-Tarnopol railway, Brzezany and on River Narajowka.

14 March Petrograd Soviet Order No. 1 – elected committees control weaponry and saluting off duty abolished. Czar's train stopped at Pskov.

17 March Russian 1st Hussars suppress a revolution in Rejitza.

19 March Petrograd Soviet appoints commissars to all units.

21 March Russian trenches near Lida (nr Vilna) taken but lost the next day.

23 March German troops massed on the Riga-Dvinsk front.

25 March Gas attack on Russian positions in the Dvinsk area is repulsed.

26 March Attack south-west of Baranovichi gains east bank of River Shchara with 300 Russian POWs.

28 March Start of spring thaw prevents large-scale fighting.

1 April Russian Army starts retreat from eastern Anatolia.

3 April In the Pripet region, General von Linsingen's troops cross the River Stokhod taking 10,000 POWs in Russian Tobol bridgehead.

14 April Thousands of deserters on the north and west fronts.

19 April All ranks of 109 Division (Twelfth Army) demand immediate peace.

22 April In the Baltic Provinces, General Hutier is made C-in-C of *Eighth Army,* replacing General Scholtz. *Army Detachment D* now commanded by Austro-Hungarian Generaloberst Graf Kirchbach.

30 April Russian positions showered with leaflets and newspapers to encourage them to desert and/or revolt.

2 May Number of Russian deserters now in the millions.

5 May On the Armenian Front, Russians withdraw from Ognot.

11 May German officers visit Russian HQ at Dvinsk. A follow-up letter suggesting an armistice is turned into a leaflet.

19 May Russian trenches near Kukhary under intense artillery fire.

1 June Localised armistice in many places while fighting continues in some areas.

9 June Russian Provisional Government refuses the unlimited armistice offer made by radio.

11 June 19th Division in Galicia moves back to Turkey.

23 June Russians issue preparatory orders for Galicia offensive.

28 June In Galicia preliminary Russian bombardment destroys Brzezany bridge.

30 June Heavy artillery barrages by both sides. German response includes gas.

1 July Russian summer offensive in Galicia starts: fifty mile front with thirty-one divisions and over thirteen hundred guns – objective Lemberg. Offensive meets with mixed fortune. Seventh Army gains little ground and loses it all to counter-attacks by 6 July. Eleventh Army drives a three-mile wedge between *Südarmee* and *Second Army*. Russians take 10,429 POWs and five guns for 17,339 casualties.

2 July In Galicia, Austrian *19 (Czech) Division* deserts en masse.

3 July Eleventh Army has taken 14,000 POWs and more than thirty guns but is unable to exploit success due to slow arrival of reserves.

6 July Eighth Army pushes *Austrian Third Army* back on whole front. Attacking south of Dniester, the Russians capture 7,000 POWs and forty-eight guns in two days. Arrival of German reserves stops Austrian rout.

9 July Austrian *Third Army* retreats to River Lomnica. Russians take 1,000 POWs.

10 July Russians take Halicz and 2,000 POWs.

11 July Town of Kalusz captured.

12 July River Lomnica crossed by Russian troops.

13 July Russians have captured 36,643 POWs.

15 July Russian eighteen-mile advance blocked by arrival of four new German divisions commanded by General Litzmann.

16 July Germans evacuate but later hold Kalusz.

18 July Litzmann's troops gain but then lose Nowica. *Army Detachment D* repels Russian attack during Battle of Dvinsk.

19 July In west Russia, *Tenth Army* repulses Russian attack after a two-mile penetration during the Battle of Smorgon-Krevo. In Galicia, preceded by a Brüchmuller hurricane barrage, a nine-division (eight from the Western Front) counter-offensive makes a twelve-mile wide breach east of Zloczow. The Russian Eleventh Army flees en masse losing 6,000 POWs and seventy guns by 21 July.

21 July In the Baltic Provinces only two of the six Russian divisions allocated to an offensive participate, one of them at gunpoint. In Galicia, German attackers near Tarnopol.

22 July Emperor Charles visits HQ at Zloczow.

23 July Russian retreat on 150-mile front. Austrian *Third Army* crosses River Lomnica and Russians give up the towns of Halicz and Stanislau.

25 July Kaiser watches *I Guard Division* take Tarnopol and cross River Sereth. Austrians retake Kolomea.

28 July In Galicia Central Powers' troops reach Russian border at Gusiatyn on River Zbruch.

29 July Russian resistance stiffens south of Dniester.

30 July Zaleszczycki and Sniatyn retaken by Austrian *Third Army*. Russian attack, assisted by RNAS armoured cars, beaten off by joint Austrian and Turkish forces near River Zbruch.

31 July Russians retreat in Czernowitz region.

1 August Russians drive *Südarmee* back across River Zbruch at Gusiatyn.

3 August Czernowitz reoccupied by *XIII Corps* (*42 Honved Infantry Division* and *5 Infantry Division*).

5 August Russian forces opposing Turks on Armenian Front start withdrawal to Europe.

19 August Germans claim 22,000 POWs in recent Galicia and Bukovina fighting.

20 August Russians evacuate some positions southwest of Riga to shorten the line. *Eighth Army* begins march on Riga for forthcoming operation.

21 August *XIII Corps* attacks Sereth, takes hill defences.

26 August *XIII Corps* continues attacks east of Czernowitz.

27 August Dolzok heights captured by *XIII Corps*.

1 September *Eighth Army* offensive at Riga begins with a two hour Brüchmuller gas shelling, causing panic and inflicting over 1,000 Russian casualties. Three divisions cross the Dvina river in pontoons covered by low-flying aircraft. In a few hours, two islands east of Riga had been stormed and a seven-mile bridgehead created. Advance halted by mid-morning.

2 September Russians evacuate Riga bridgehead and Riga.

3 September *1 Reserve* and *2 Guard Division* enter Riga. Russians hold on to positions south of highway and railway.

4 September Russian counter-attack fails to stop German advance.

6 September Kaiser visits Riga and reviews troops.

13 September Germans evacuate Gusiatyn on Russian border.

18 September National Council of Lithuania demands independence.

19 September Latvian Brigade repulses German attacks east of Riga.

20 September Russians defeat Turks near Ortobo.

21 September Bridgehead on Dvina at Jakobstadt, held since October 1915, evacuated by Russians. *Eighth Army* take 4,000 POWs and fifty guns for 700 casualties. Courland claims independence from Russia and requests German protection.

26 September Remaining Turkish units leave Galicia for Istanbul. No Turkish troops left in Galicia.

3 October In the Baltic Provinces, an intense artillery duel at Jakobstadt. Russian guns halt attack near the Romanian border.

4 October Renewed British pressure in Flanders forces transfer of five divisions from Riga to the Western Front. Russians repulse attacks east of Riga.

6 October South of Czernowitz, after heavy fighting, Russians take 750 POWs.

9 October In the Pripet region, Emperor Charles reviews troops in Kovel.

11 October Russians relinquish ground near Segewold in Latvia.

12 October Operation Albion commences: landing of General Kathen's *42 Infantry Division* on the Gulf of Riga islands. Troops ashore in five hours.

13 October Capital of Oesel Island, Arensburg, occupied, but troops fail to land on Dagö Island.

14 October Defending Russians cut-off on Svorbe peninsula with no escape. Island secured with 10,000 POWs and fifty guns.

16 October Russian citizens evacuate Reval in Estonia.

17 October Russians repulse attempted landing on Dagö Island in Gulf of Riga.

18 October Russians evacuate Moon Island in the Gulf of Riga.

19 October German marines take Dagö Island.

20 October Dagö and Schildau Island both secured by German troops.

21 October Russians repulse some of the attacks on mainland Estonia but landing force takes and holds Verder. Germans claim to have had only fifty-four soldiers killed and have captured over 20,000 POWs and over 140 guns since the start of Operation Albion.

23 October Russians follow up German troops who retired over twenty miles to shorten the line since the night of 21/22 October from positions northeast of Riga.

27 October Landing force evacuate Verder.

29 October Attack on Russian positions in the Janinzen-Skuli sector is repulsed.

21 November Bolsheviks radio C-in-C Dukhonin to negotiate an armistice.

22 November Dukhonin sacked for not negotiating and replaced by Ensign Kirilenko.

25 November Fraternisation between troops near Baranovichi.

27 November Armistice delegates return with German consent in principle. Next meeting scheduled for 1 December.

28 November Estonia declares independence from Russia.

2 December Ceasefire begins on dates fixed by local army commanders. Russian armistice commission crosses line at Dvinsk and moves on to Brest-Litovsk. Met and welcomed by Prince Leopold, C-in-C of German forces.

3 December Talks begin between Russia and all the Central Powers.

7 December Official truce between Russia and Central Powers.

8 December All hostilities suspended.

9 December Finland demands all Russian troops leave.

11 December Lithuania proclaims independence.

12 December General Graf Kirchbach takes over command of *Eighth Army*, replacing Hutier who is moved to the Western Front.

13 December Armistice negotiations resume.

15 December Brest-Litovsk twenty-eight day armistice signed between Russia and Central Powers. Begins at noon on 17 December. A week's notice needed to terminate agreement. Germans given police powers in Baltic countries.

16 December Turkish *Caucasus Army Group* dissolved.

17 December Armistice to start at noon.

18 December Ceasefire agreed between Turkey and the newly independent Trans-Caucasian Republic.

22 December Brest-Litovsk peace negotiations begin.

26 December Bolsheviks break off talks when told Poland and Baltic states will become independent.

27 December Latvia declares independence and asks for German protection.

29 December Discussions on technical details of the armistice begin in Petrograd.

1918

6 January Finland's independence recognised by Germany.

8 January Brest-Litovsk talks continue.

10 January Bolsheviks and Central Powers recognise Ukraine as an independent state.

12 January Latvia declares independence.

23 January Brest-Litovsk talks suspended. Enver Paşa orders the Third Army to commence a new offensive at the Caucasus front.

25 January *Südarmee* disbanded.

26 January Ukraine declares independence.

28 January Germans invited to occupy Estonia.

30 January Brest-Litovsk talks resume.

1 February Central Powers recognise Ukrainian independence. German divisions start to transfer to the Western Front.

7 February The Kaiser orders Kühlmann to end the Brest-Litovsk talks and demand control of the Baltic states.

9 February Central Powers sign separate peace with the Ukraine.

10 February Talks break down for the fourth time.

12 February Turkish forces capture Cardakli in eastern Anatolia from the Russians.

13 February 'Bad Homburg Crown Council decides on further advance into Russia with the Kaiser demanding that the Russians be beaten to death'.

14 February Turks capture Erzincan from the Russians.

16 February Lithuania declares independence from Russia. Russians threatened that the armistice will end at noon on 18 February.

17 February Ukrainians ask for German help against the Reds.

18 February Peace conditions accepted by Reds after Operation Faustschlag starts. German troops advance along railway lines taking Dvinsk and Lutsk.

20 February Operation Faustschlag continues with the capture of Minsk and Hapsal.

21 February Advance continues with capture of Rechitsa.

23 February Bolsheviks agree to evacuate Finland. Peace terms become stiffer.

24 February Borisov and Dorpat in Estonia taken and Estonia proclaims independence. Soviets accept new peace terms. Turkish *36 Division* near Erzerum and Turkish *II Caucasian Corps* reoccupies Gümüsane and Trabzon.

25 February General Linsingen's troops reach Zhitomir in the Ukraine. Turkish forces capture Trabzon from the Russians.

26 February The *Baltic See Division* (*12 Landwehr*) designated for use in Finnish intervention to be commanded by Major-General Graf von der Goltz.

28 February Central Powers continue their attacks in the Ukraine. 900 troops leave Danzig for the Aaland Islands in Finland.

1 March German troops occupy Polotsk, Bobruisk, Gomel and Mohilev. More divisions released for the Western Front.

2 March Linsingen's force captures Kiev. German troops land on Aaland Island.

3 March Russo-German Peace of Brest-Litovsk: Russia cedes three Armenian districts to Turkey, and renounces the Baltic States, Belorussia, Finland and Poland. 630,000 Austrian POWs to be returned home but fighting continues. German advance ordered to halt except in the Ukraine.

5 March Returning from Palestine, Falkenhayn takes command of *Tenth Army*.

12 March Linsingen's troops occupy Odessa. Turks retake Erzerum.

14 March Peace treaty ratified in Moscow.

17 March German *LII.Korps* continues its advance, capturing Nikolayev in the Ukraine.

21 March Forty-two German divisions still in Russia with nearly 700,000 men.

23 March Lithuania recognised as an independent state by Germany. Turkish forces capture Malazgirt from the Russians.

25 March Turkish troops cross the pre-war Turkish-Russian border.

29 March In the Ukraine, Poltava is occupied by *2 Cavalry Division*.

31 March *Army Group Eichhorn*, eighteen divisions, formed at Kiev to occupy the Ukraine. *Bugarmee* dissolved and General von Linsingen removed to become Military Governor of Berlin.

1 April Eight divisions transferred to the Western Front. *Baltic Division* sails from Danzig for Finland.

3 April Over 9,000 German troops land at Hangö in Finland. Fighting in the Ukraine continues with Germans taking Ekaterinoslav.

5 April Kharkov occupied. Turkish forces capture Sarıkamış from the Russians and reoccupy Van.

6 April Turkish forces capture Van from the Russians.

7 April German landing at Lovisa (Finland) unopposed.

9 April Turks attack positions at Batumi.

10 April In continued fighting Germans take Kherson and Belgograd.

13 April Germans take Helsinki for 200 casualties.

14 April Turkish troops capture Dogubeyazıt from the Russians and liberate Batumi.

19 April Crimea invaded and Simferopol occupied by Germans. Armenian line southwest of Kars broken by Turkish *I Caucasian Corps*.

24 April Red Guards fail to take Lahti (Finland) from Germans.

25 April Turkish forces retake Kars from the Russians.

26 April Germans capture Hämeenlinna and meet up with Finnish troops.

28 April Germans reach Taganrog on the Sea of Azov. In night fighting, Red Guards throw German troops back near Lahti, but town holds out.

29 April Military dictatorship established in the Ukraine.

30 April 386,000 Austrian and German POWs returned home.

1 May Part of Black Sea Fleet seized during German occupation of Sevastopol. Two German divisions transfer to the Western Front.

8 May Rostov occupied by Germans.

11 May Germans agree to send some men to the Caucasus.

15 May Although involved in peace talks, the Turks resume their offensive and take Aleksandropol.

18 May Turkish *12 Division* attacks south of the River Aras.

19 May Two passes on the Tiflis road captured by Turkish *5 Division*.

20 May With war in Finland over, new Finnish Army to be modelled on German Army with German troops remaining.

21 May Turkish *9* and *36 Divisions* throw back Armenians from Amamli Station.

23 May Turkish *11 Division* pushed back thirty miles.

25 May Turkish attack on Armenian positions north of Erevan fails.

3 June Two German battalions from *217 Division* land at Poti in Georgia.

4 June Duke of Württemberg accepts the throne of Lithuania.

7 June On the Don, German troops occupy Bataisk.

10 June Turkish *9 Caucasian Division* clashes with combined German-Georgian forces at Vorontsovka and pushes it back.

12 June In Georgia, Germans occupy Tiflis.

14 June Fighting continues in south Russia, near Taganrog.

17 June Austrians take 100,000 POWs in the Ukraine.

20 June Turkish *5 Caucasian Division* arrives at Elizavetpol in newly independent Azerbaijan as main unit in the Army of Islam.

29 June In Azerbaijan, Azeri Tartars and Turks attack and defeat eight Armenian battalions near Gök-çay.

30 June Over 500,000 Austrian and German POWs now repatriated.

1 July Estonia proclaims independence and rejects German aid. Armenians retreat in Azerbaijan.

6 July German Ambassador in Moscow murdered by two members of the Left Socialist Revolutionary Party.

11 July Prince William of Urach becomes King Mindove II of Lithuania.

16 July Imperial Family murdered at Ekaterinburg and five Princes killed in Alapaevsk.

19 July Nakhichevan in Azerbaijan captured from Russians.

30 July In the Ukraine, Feldmarschall Eichhorn and Captain Dressler are murdered by a Left Socialist Revolutionary Party bomb. General Kirnbach succeeds Eichhorn as C-in-C *Army Group Kiev*, who in turn is replaced as C-in-C *Eighth Army* by General von Kathen.

5 August Turkish attack on Baku repulsed. In Georgia Germans hamper munitions shipments to the Turks.

9 August Thirty-seven German divisions still in Russia.

26 August Turks overrun British positions on Mud Volcano at Baku.

27 August Germany and Russia sign supplementary Peace Treaty. German troops to stop Finns attacking Russia so that Russians can oppose North Russia landings by the Allies. Russia to pay £300 million more in reparations and allow Germans use of the Black Sea Fleet. When Baku is returned by the Turks, Russia agrees to provide 1/3rd of her oil to Germany.

1 September Austrian *106 Infantry Division* and three German divisions leave for the Western Front. Turks take Digya north of Baku.

14 September Germans offer not to attack in East Karelia (bordering Finland) if Allies evacuate north Russia. Turks capture Wolf's Gate in Baku.

15 September Turkish troops enter Baku.

20 September Russo-Turkish treaty repudiated.

1 October Four more German divisions transferred to the Western Front. Germans release Russian POWs to newly formed White Russian Northern Corps.

2 October *Armeeabteilung D* disbanded.

4 October In Galicia, German-aided Ukrainians attack Poles.

28 October Army of Islam captures Petrovsk in the last successful Turkish offensive of the war. Turkish forces reach their northernmost point in the Caucasus.

1 November Two German divisions transferred to the Western Front.

3 November Ukrainians seize Czernowitz in the Bukovina.

8 November Poland informs Austria that they have assumed sovereignty over Galicia.

11 November Twenty-six German divisions spread across a front from Finland to Georgia and seven Austrian divisions in the Ukraine.

16 November German evacuation of the Ukraine begins and four divisions leave Finland.

17 November British and White Russians reoccupy Baku.

16 December Remaining German troops leave Finland.

17 December All Turkish troops back at the 1877 frontier.

18 December Germans evacuate Dorpat in Estonia.

Bibliography

Asprey, R. The German High Command at War. William Morrow & Co. 1991.

Baer. C H. Der Völkerkrieg. Julius Hoffmann. Various dates.

Beckett, I.F.W. The Great War (2nd edition). Pearson. 2007.

Bradley, J. Allied intervention in Russia 1917-1920. Weidenfeld & Nicholson. 1968.

Bull, S. German Assault troops of the First World War. Spellmount. 2007.

Chickering, R. Imperial Germany and the Great War, 1914-1918. Cambridge University Press, 2005.

De Groot, G.J. The First World War. Palgrave Macmillan. 2001.

Dowling, T.C. The Brusilov offensive. Indiana University Press. 2008.

Edmonds, Brigadier General Sir James, CB, CMG. Military Operations France & Belgium 1914. Macmillan & Co, 1922.

Edmonds, Brigadier General Sir James, CB, CMG. Military Operations France & Belgium 1915, volume 2. Macmillan & Co, 1928.

Edmonds, Brigadier General Sir James, CB, CMG. Military Operations France & Belgium 1918, volume 1. Macmillan & Co. 1935.

Ellis, J & Cox M. The World War 1 databook. Aurum Press. 2001.

Falls, Captain C. Military Operations France & Belgium 1917. The German retreat to the Hindenburg line and the battle of Arras. Macmillan. 1940.

Foley, R. German strategy and the path to Verdun. University Press Cambridge. 2005.

Gatrell, P. Russia's first World War. Longman. 2005.

Gray, R & Argyle, C. Chronicle of the First World War Volume 1, 1914 – 1916. Facts on File, 1991.

Gray, R & Argyle, C. Chronicle of the First World War Volume 2, 1917 – 1921. Facts on File, 1991.

Herwig, H. The First World War, Germany and Austria 1914-1918. Arnold, Headline Group. 1997.

http://www.gwpda.org/   Great War Primary Documents Archive.

http://www.turkeyswar.com/index.html

Kriegs Invaliden Hilfe. Taschen-Atlas der Kriegsschauplätze. Verlags Aktiengesellschaft. 1916.

Ludendorff, General. My War Memories 1914-1918 volume 1 & 2. Hutchinson. (No Date).

Miles, W. Military Operations France and Belgium, 1916 volume 2. Macmillan & Co. 1938.

Ministry of Information. Chronology of the war. Constable & Co. Ltd. 1919.

Morse, J. An Englishman in the Russian Ranks. Nonsuch Publishing. 2006.

Neiberg, S. & Jordan, D. The Eastern Front 1914-1920. Amber Books. 2008.

Rachamimov, A. POWs and the Great War. Berg. 2002.

Rutherford, W. The Russian Army in World War 1. Gordon Cremonosi Publishers. 1975.

Scarlata, P. Austro-Hungarian rifles of World War 1. The Armourer Issue 115. 2013.

Schulte, K. Der Grosse Krieg in Bildern. Verlag Georg Stilke. Various dates.

Staff, G. Battle for the Baltic Islands 1917. Pen & Sword Maritime. 2008.

Stoff, L.S. They fought for the Motherland. University of Kansas. 2006.

Stevenson, D. The History of the First World War. Allen Lane. 2004.

Stevenson, D. With our backs to the wall. Penguin. 2012.

Stone, N. The Eastern Front 1914-1917. Hodder and Stoughton. 1975.

Thoumin, R. The First World War. Secker & Warburg. 1963.

Tunstall, G.A. Blood on the snow. University Press of Kansas. 2010.

Unknown. Grosser Bilder Atlas des Weltkrieges. Verlag von F Bruckmann. Various dates.

Watson, A. Enduring the Great War. Cambridge University Press. 2008.

Witkop, P (Ed.). German students' war letters. Pine Street Books. 2002.